Governing London: Competitiveness and Regeneration for a Global City

Middlesex University Research Materials

Governing London: Competitiveness and Regeneration for a Global City

Edited by
Stephen Syrett and Robert Baldock

Centre for Enterprise and Economic
Development Research (CEEDR)
Middlesex University

Middlesex University Press
London

First published in 2001 by Middlesex University Press

Middlesex University Press is an imprint of
Middlesex University Services Limited,
Bounds Green Road, London N11 2NQ

A CIP catalogue record for this book is available from
The British Library

ISBN 1 898253 45 5

Cover design by Helen Taylor

Manufacture coordinated in UK from Editors CRC by
Book-in-Hand Limited.

Contents

List of Figures and Tables

Figures

Tables

List of Contributors

Nick Bailey

Nick Bailey is Chair of the Department of Planning and Urban Design at the University of Westminster and in 1996 set up the University's Masters programme in Urban Regeneration. After qualifying as a town planner, he has worked for several London Boroughs in both housing and planning departments. He has also worked closely with the community sector and is currently Chair of the Fitzrovia Trust. He has carried out research for the DoE on development trusts and has written extensively on planning and urban regeneration in London. He is co-author of *Partnership Agencies in British Urban Policy* (1995), UCL Press: London.

Robert Baldock

Rob Baldock is Principal Researcher at the Centre for Enterprise and Economic Development Research (CEEDR), Middlesex University Business School. He has published several articles on economic regeneration policy in London including: *Ten Years of the Urban Programme 1981-91: The Impact and implications of its Assistance to Small Businesses* (Urban Studies, 1998); and *From Crisis Manager to Strategic Partner: The Changing Role of Four London Boroughs in Economic Regeneration* (with Professor David North, Town Planning Review, 2000).

Paul Benneworth

Paul Benneworth is a Research Associate at the Centre for Urban and Regional Development Studies (CURDS) at Newcastle University. He has a core interest in knowledge, learning and regional governance. Paul is also a regular contributor on the topic of RDAs to *Regions*, the Regional Studies Association Newsletter, and a collection of these essays, including a chapter on London, is being published by the Association in 2001.

David Charles

David Charles is a Principal Research Associate at the Centre for Urban and Regional Development Studies (CURDS) at Newcastle University. He has a wide range of research interests which include the role of universities in regional development, corporate restructuring, regional technology policy and urban development. He recently co-ordinated a major European Framework project on universities and regional development (UNIREG), and has been working on a range of other research projects on universities and innovation policy, economic clusters (for the OECD and DETR), and the role of cities in regional competitiveness.

Greg Clark

Greg Clark is Managing Director, of Economic Development at Greater London Enterprise Ltd., the regional development company owned by London's 33 municipalities. He is an emerging leader, on the practitioner side, and has extensive experience of UK, European and North American approaches to urban, local, and regional economic development through his work in economic development and urban regeneration in London over the last 15 years. Greg is a non-executive director of the European Association of Development Agencies (EURADA) (and Chair of their Urban Development Agencies grouping), the British Urban Regeneration Association, Vision for London, the Unemployment Unit and Youthaid. He is a frequent speaker and media commentator and member of OECD evaluation teams on local and regional development and urban regeneration. As a Harkness Fellow in 1995, he spent a year in the USA assessing economic development agencies in American and Canadian cities and regions. He has authored a number of reports comparing urban economic development in Britain, Europe and the USA. He is a visiting Professor at London Guildhall University and a Fellow of the Royal Society of Arts.

Bob Colenutt

Bob Colenutt worked for community groups on the South Bank and in Docklands between 1972-84. He was at the GLC between 1984-86 and was head of the Docklands Consultative Committee Support Unit between 1986-92. He was a councillor at the London Borough of Lambeth between 1986-90. He was head of the Thames Gateway Unit at the London Borough of Barking and Dagenham between 1992-94 and joined the London Borough of Haringey in 1994, where he is currently Head of Policy and Regeneration.

Ram Gidoomal

Made a CBE in 1998 for services to the Asian Business Community and Race Relations, Ram Gidoomal is a member of the Government appointed and independent 'Better Regulation Task Force' for which he chairs the Anti-Discrimination Sub Group. He is a non executive director of the Epsom & St Helier NHS Trust. He was a founder of the Christmas Cracker project, which has given thousands of young people direct entrepreneurial experience and which has raised over £5 million for charity. As well as being a frequent media commentator, Ram is on the Board of Business Link's National Accreditation Advisory Board and is also the author of several books including *Sari 'n' Chips*, *The UK Maharajahs* and the research report *The £5 billion South Asian Corridor*. He is a governor of two schools, business advisor to the Prince's Youth Business Trust, Chairman of South Asian Development Partnership and a patron of the Small Business Bureau.

Ian Gordon

Ian Gordon is Professor of Human Geography at the London School of Economics and is currently directing (with Nick Buck, Peter Hall, Michael Harloe and Mark Kleinman) an ESRC funded study entitled *London: Economic Competitiveness, Social Cohesion and the Policy Environment*. His principal research interests are in urban economies, labour markets and policies. Publications from previous studies include *The London Employment Problem* (with Nick Buck and Ken Young), *Divided Cities: New York and London in the Contemporary World*, and *Territorial Competition in an Integrating Europe* (with Paul Cheshire).

Susanne MacGregor

Susanne MacGregor is Professor of Social Policy at Middlesex University. Publications include: *Tackling the Inner Cities* (edited with Ben Pimlott) (1990) Clarendon Press: Oxford; *The Other City: People and Politics in New York and London* (edited with Arthur Lipow) (1995) Humanities Press: New Jersey; *Transforming Cities: Contested Governance and New Spatial Divisions* (edited with Nick Jewson) (1997); and *Social Issues and Party Politics* (edited with Helen Jones) (1998) Routledge: London.

Peter Newman

Peter Newman is Senior Lecturer in the School of the Built Environment, University of Westminster. His recent research includes studies of European urban planning (*Urban Planning in Europe* (1996), Routledge), the changing nature of London governance, and comparative studies of approaches to urban revitalisation. He is currently involved in three research projects: a comparison of the governance of European city regions, a set of studies of urban planning and city management issues in 'world cities' (book to be published by Macmillan in 2002), and research into the development of new tourism areas in London.

Eric Sorenson

Eric Sorensen was the Chief Executive of the London Development Partnership during its two year existence from 1998 to June 2000. He has considerable experience in the development and regeneration fields, and for many years was a civil servant in the Department of Environment (now DETR) dealing with urban policy and housing issues. Four years were spent as the Departmental Regional Director for the North West with responsibility for setting up a wide range of community and regeneration projects in Merseyside. Subsequently, he left the Department to become Chief Executive of the London Docklands Development Corporation in 1991 and worked there for six years. He was then appointed Chief Executive of the Millennium Commission and left the Commission in 1999.

Stephen Syrett

Stephen Syrett is Principal Lecturer in the School of Social Science at Middlesex University and member of the university's Centre for Enterprise and Economic Development Research (CEEDR). His research interests relate to issues of urban regeneration and local and regional development. Current research projects include work on changing forms of economic governance in London and Lisbon and an EU funded study on the role of social capital in local economic development. He is the Programme Leader for the MA Local Economic Development and the Postgraduate Certificate in Citizenship, Culture and Leadership. He had published widely in this field including *Local Development* (1995) as well as more broadly on Portugal, *Contemporary Portugal* (2001).

Andrew Thornley

Andy Thornley is Director of Planning Studies at the LSE. His interest is in the relationship between politics and urban planning. His recent books include *Urban Planning under Thatcherism* (1993), *The Crisis of London* (1992), and *Urban Planning in Europe: International Competition, National Systems and Planning Projects* (1996) (with Peter Newman). He is currently working on a book about urban planning in World Cities and an ESRC research project which explores the agenda setting stage of the GLA with a focus on planning and sustainability.

Acknowledgements

This book draws upon research funded by Middlesex University under the Non Formula Funded Research (NFFR) programme into *City Governance in a Global Economy*. The conference held in February 2000 from which this book emerged was also supported by NFFR funds (Mode 1) as part of Middlesex University's *Regional Regeneration Research Programme*. In organising the original conference and in preparing this book a number of staff from the Centre for Enterprise and Economic Development Research (CEEDR) have provided valuable assistance, support and advice. We would particularly like to thank David North, Sue Engelbert, Amanda Stack, Pamela Macaulay and Steven Burgess, for all their efforts. We would also like to thank Steve Chilton and Yvette Brown from the Technical Unit of the School of Social Science for preparing figures and diagrams, and Ra'ana Haider and Marion Locke from Middlesex University Press for their patience and help in getting the book to publication.

Preface

This book emerged out of a one day conference organised by Middlesex University's Centre for Enterprise and Economic Development Research, which took place at the university's Trent Park Campus on 4th February 2000. This conference, entitled *Governing London: Competitiveness and Regeneration for a Global City*, looked towards approaching changes in the governance of economic development and regeneration activity within London. The forthcoming election of a Mayor and Assembly and the creation of the Greater London Authority (in May 2000) and the new Mayoral economic development agency (the London Development Agency) (in July 2000), provided the context for debate. Contributions from a mix of academics and practitioners identified the major economic development and regeneration challenges faced by London and the extent to which proposed changes in the system of economic governance were appropriate to these challenges.

The contributions contained in this volume combine fully revised and updated versions of papers presented at the original conference along with a number of additionally commissioned papers. The volume retains a mix of papers from academics and practitioners and the original focus on the multi-faceted nature of the economic governance issues which London currently faces. What is manifest in this period of fast moving change is that there is no masterplan for the governance of economic development within London. Rather what is unfolding is an evolving and messy process set within a fluid and dynamic broader environment. This edited collection aims to contribute to this process by stimulating debate concerning how to promote and manage economic development and regeneration in a manner that will benefit all of the people of London.

Stephen Syrett and Rob Baldock
London, March 2001

Chapter 1

Changing Times, Changing Styles: New Forms of Economic Governance in London

STEPHEN SYRETT AND ROBERT BALDOCK

Introduction

These are interesting times in the development of London's governance. After fourteen years without a strategic authority, the establishment of an elected Mayor and Assembly in May 2000 marked the beginning of a new phase in London's government system. For economic development and regeneration activity these changes appear particularly important. As part of the process that established the Greater London Authority (GLA) a new Mayoral agency, the London Development Agency (LDA), officially came into existence in July 2000 to take the lead role for economic development and regeneration activity. Furthermore, as a result of changes in central government policy to the institutional infrastructures delivering post-16 education and training and business support, from April 2001 five local Learning and Skills Councils (LSCs) and a new Small Business Service (SBS) also came into operation in London. These combined changes ensure that the future economic governance of London will be characterised by a number of important new economic development institutions and a key role for the elected Mayor.

Yet the significance of these changes remains unclear. Devolution of power to London appeared later on the political agenda than was the case for Scotland and Wales, a factor that limited the extent of debate concerning the nature and process of devolution in London. The GLA Act (1999) that established the Authority and Functional Bodies, a long and complex piece of legislation, is notably vague on the responsibilities of different institutions and agencies and how they will operate in practice. The

1

current period is thus one of particular importance. The ways of working and the nature of institutional relationships currently being established will be critical in structuring the future development of London's system of economic governance.

Recent changes raise hard questions concerning whether the emerging institutional framework will be any better placed to deliver the current 'holy trinity' of economic development and regeneration policy: economic competitiveness, social cohesion and environmental sustainability. Will the new institutions merely add another layer of organisation on top of the already overcrowded institutional structure of London? Or will they genuinely be able to make a difference through introducing greater strategic vision, integration and co-ordination of action? Will the Mayor, GLA and related agencies have sufficient political and economic power to effect change, or does the hand of central government still rest heavy on the key levers of economic power? Are the governance structures currently being put in place in London appropriate to the needs of a leading world city within a globalising economy? Are they capable of both enhancing London's global competitiveness but also tackling the severe problems of localised multiple deprivation which are such a distinctive feature of London's current economic landscape?

To begin to answer these questions requires consideration of wider changes in governance structures and the shift towards new forms of multi-level, multi-nodal and multinational networked governance, which cut across different policy levels (supranational, national, regional, local) and sectors (public, private, voluntary, community) (Benington & Harvey, 1998). Analysis of processes of change in London's economic governance structures is therefore of interest to other major cities within the UK, where the potential role of Mayors and new forms of city-region governance is currently under active consideration, and internationally, where other world cities face similar challenges of promoting global economic competitiveness whilst managing rising social inequality and increasing environmental degradation. Does London provide an emerging model for other city-regions of how, or indeed how not to, manage processes of economic development and regeneration?

Taking the current period of institutional change as its starting point, this book explores the nature of the governance challenges presented by economic development and regeneration within London. Through looking outward to experiences internationally and inward to the particular economic and political structures within London, the book identifies key problems with the existing system of governance which has evolved over the last twenty years, and begins to identify what changes are needed to ensure more effective, inclusive and democratic governance in the future. The rest of this introductory chapter examines the context from which current changes in London's economic governance have emerged: first, through consideration of the forces that led to current changes in London's governance; and second, via analysis of the economic governance system that emerged in the post 1986 period and the problems associated with it. The chapter then considers some of the new economic institutions within London particularly focusing on the LDA given its key role in leading and co-ordinating economic development activity. The final section outlines the structure of the book and introduces the subsequent contributions.

Contexts for Change: London and the 'New Regionalism'

After over twenty years in which issues of devolution and regional planning received scant attention from politicians and policy makers in the UK, the latter part of the 1990s witnessed a revived interest in the regional dimension. Whilst in the 1980s the Conservative administration actively dismantled existing regional economic planning frameworks and adopted a 'pro-Union' view of Britain, the Labour government of 1997 came to power with a well developed regional agenda. The emergence of the so-called 'new regionalism' was driven by a number of interrelated factors: recognition of the growing importance of regional competitiveness in a globalising economy; the increasing fragmentation in the forms of sub-national governance; and a desire to promote greater political devolution and new forms of political mobilisation. It is within this broad context that recent changes in the governance of economic development within London need to be understood.

Regional competitiveness in a global economy

Analyses of processes of economic globalisation commonly point to the increasing importance of the region and the reduced primacy of the nation state as the key economic unit within the global economy (e.g. Scott, 1998; Storper, 1997; Krugman, 1991). Whilst such arguments remain strongly contested, there can be no doubt that the re-emergence of the region as an important economic unit has been influential in focusing discussion on the nature and type of regional level governance necessary for ensuring regional competitiveness. Much of this debate has focused on certain powerhouse regions, the technology districts, global cities and new industrial districts, which appear to play a key role in driving forward the development of a global economy. A defining feature of these regions, it is argued, is their ability to learn and adapt to change in response to increasing flows of information and a rapidly changing external economic environment (Cooke and Morgan, 1998). This ability appears to be largely rooted within the institutions and governance structures of a region and hence regional policy formulation has increasingly shifted attention towards creating flexible, networked regional governance systems capable of 'capturing' global processes of changes.

Within the UK, and particularly the English context, the absence of existing, strong, regionally based structures has limited the potential for strategies promoting regional economic competitiveness. The need for more sophisticated and co-ordinated approaches to attracting inward investment did lead to the development of regionally based inward investment agencies such as London First. Yet such ad-hoc business led agencies were poorly positioned to integrate inward investment policies with other areas of business support policy, or indeed with wider regeneration policies. During the 1990s the Labour party, whilst in opposition, began to develop an agenda amenable to the support of policies promoting regional economic competitiveness. With clear evidence of continuing regional disparities, potential policy solutions which promoted strong regional economies through better integrated and more democratic, regionally based governance systems gained momentum. The 1992 Labour party manifesto recognised that the ability of London to compete globally was being hampered by the lack of city-wide strategic governance and subsequent reports similarly concluded that competitiveness in the English regions was being constrained by the lack of single, strategic regional development agencies (RPC, 1996: CBI, 1997). The eventual creation by the Labour government of the Regional Development Agencies (RDAs) in the 1998 RDA Act was therefore informed, at least in part, by an economic case; one that sought to tackle persistent regional inequalities and create a series of powerful regional economies within the UK capable of competing within a globalising economy.

Complexity and fragmentation in local and regional governance

Sub-national economic governance in Britain during the 1980s and 1990s was characterised by strong central government control and an emphasis on local level delivery involving an ever expanding range of locally and regionally based, non-elected actors. The proliferation of quasi public/private sector organisations (such as Training and Enterprise Councils and Business Links) and partnership based delivery of economic regeneration policies led to increasing fragmentation and complexity as well as competition between local and regional partnerships for central government and European funding. The ongoing failure of economic regeneration policy to address the combination of factors (e.g. poor housing, education, health facilities and public transport) which continued to afflict deprived areas, and the lack of co-ordination and co-operation between agencies and programmes operating within the same geographical areas, led to calls for a more coherent and strategic approach to urban policy (Robson et al, 1994). The need for greater co-ordination and strategic approaches development activities at the region and city-wide level was further reinforced by the requirements of EU regional policy, where greater institutional coherence in the UK was necessary in order to realise maximum benefits from the Structural Funds (Newman, 2000; and see chapter 3).

Recognition by central government of the need for greater policy integration and coherence led to the launch of 10 Government Offices for the Regions (GORs) in 1994 (Mawson, 1997). The GORs sought to co-ordinate regional activity across various government departments (Department of Trade and Industry (DTI), Department of the Environment (DoE), Department of Transport (DT), and Department of Employment (DE)) and were given strategic control over the key central government urban policy tool for local regeneration, the Single Regeneration Budget (SRB), as well as responsibility for managing European Structural Funds. However, the GORs, staffed by civil servants and accountable to central government, lacked accountability to the regions they served and credibility with other locally and regionally based organisations. A major objective of the regional agenda of the incoming Labour administration in 1997 was therefore to provide a 'joined-up' strategic approach to the disjointed situation of urban and regional policy prevalent in the late 1990s. The major tool for achieving this were the RDAs which marked: "..the realisation that the ad hoc style of regional administration that operated in England from the late 1970s to the late 1990s was fragmented, often inefficient, sometimes confused and always unaccountable" (Roberts, 1999: p.112).

Devolution and political mobilisation

In the 1980s and 1990s, falling turn outs in national and local elections and the prolonged lack of electoral legitimacy of successive Conservative governments in Scotland and Wales, reignited the desire for political devolution as well as concerns that government had become disconnected from voters. These fears of a growing 'democratic deficit', led the opposition Labour Party to draw up proposals for significant changes in regional and local government. Alongside proposals for the establishment of assemblies in Scotland and Wales, the Labour Party's consultation document, *A Choice for England* published in 1995, also recommended the formation of regional assemblies with limited powers within England. To achieve integration of these democratically accountable regional assemblies with regional economic and social policy, a further report (RPC, 1996) recommended the establishment of Regional Development Agencies (RDAs) as the executive arm for the regional assemblies. At the local level, proposals for the reform of local government focused on improving the quality of service delivery and seeking to encourage greater public participation and democratic accountability.

On coming to power in May 1997, the new Labour government set about pursuing its particular vision of governance in the English regions. The newly created Department of the Environment, Transport and the Regions (DETR) headed by the Deputy Prime Minister John Prescott, published the RDA Bill in 1998 and eight RDAs (excluding London) were formally established in April 1999. Significantly, the RDA Bill had no provision for directly elected assemblies thus removing the link originally envisaged to democratically accountable regional assemblies (Mawson, 1999). In July 1997 a consultation paper setting out proposals for the creation of a Greater London Authority (GLA) with an elected Mayor was also published (DETR, 1997). The suggestion for an elected Mayor to provide 'leadership and a voice for London' was a radical departure from previous government reforms in London. Driven by the principle that London could benefit from an American style city Mayor to promote it on the global stage, it also represented a move towards a new style of city and municipal leadership which it was hoped would foster renewed interest in local/regional government (Hambleton and Sweeting, 1999). In London, the RDA, called the London Development Agency (LDA), was linked into the new political structures for London, and came into existence officially in July 2000. The selection of London as the first English region to get an elected Assembly marked recognition of the increasingly anomalous position of a major world city lacking its own elected authority. However it also reflected practical considerations, given that it was a fairly simple task to restore a regional tier of governance to an existing unitary local government structure co-terminus with the Greater London area boundary (Benneworth, 1999a).

Fragmentary Governance: 1986-2000

Since the politically motivated abolition of the Greater London Council (GLC) by the Conservative administration in 1986, London operated in the absence of any elected strategic authority[1]. The system of governance that subsequently developed was characterised by a complex web of multiple and overlapping institutions, lacking in strategic co-ordination and democratic accountability (Newman & Thornley, 1997; Hebbert, 1995, Bailey, 1997). As elsewhere in the UK, this system was characterised by contestation, most notably between local and central government, but also between local authorities and a variety of quasi-governmental agencies involved in economic regeneration (Stewart, 1994, Lloyd and Meegan, 1996).

The failure of London's governance system to deliver an integrated and co-ordinated response to its economic and social need was rooted within a number of factors (Bailey, 1997). First, there was a lack of any strategic vision, largely because of the absence of any single institution with the necessary credibility to co-ordinate and promote an economic development vision for London. The actions of GOL, the one organisation charged with a strategic role, have been generally pragmatic and short-termist. Their lack of direct accountability to London's population has meant it has lacked legitimacy in the eyes of other London based agencies and institutions. Although GOL administered a wide range of regeneration programmes, including the flagship SRB, it was never required to locate these within any overall regional strategy for London. Alternative public-private partnerships, such as the London Pride Partnership[2], which did begin to develop a vision for London in the 1990s, had broader based support, but still lacked the necessary institutional structures and democratic legitimacy to carry this vision forward (Newman, 1995).

Second, London has suffered from a lack of policy integration. Bailey (1997: p.210) describes how the urban policy field within London in the 1990s resulted in "a complex multi-layering of activity, duplication and confusion". Although GOL took over the function of integrating policy after 1994, considerable overlap existed between their powers and those of private sector-led agencies promoting London (such as London First and the

London Pride Partnership) and LPAC and the London TEC Council. Furthermore, the activities of several major government departments and inward investment agencies remained largely outside of GOL's control and thus militated against the creation of integrated economic development policy.

Third, conflicts over boundaries of operation emerged as a result of strong competition between sub-regional partnerships for national and EU public funding and private sector inward investment. Across London, areas such as Park Royal, Lee Valley, Wandle Valley, Greenwich Waterfront and Thames Gateway were all competing against each other for public and private investment funds. In contrast, other areas, including the strategically important central London area, remained divided between several boroughs with no single agency responsible for their co-ordination. The result was considerable waste of resources in competitive bidding across London, and a narrow focus on sub-regional and local scales at the expense of the wider pan-London interests.

Finally, the abolition of the GLC removed a major link between political accountability and the economic regeneration process in London. In the ensuing period a wide range of local authority regeneration activity was transferred to non-elected government appointed bodies such as TECs and Business Links (see Table 1.1), thus further removing the traditional links between economic development and representative democracy within London (North & Baldock, 2000). Although the development of partnership working throughout the 1990s did bring a wider range of groups into the regeneration process, the complexity and fragmentary nature of such arrangements ensured that links between economic regeneration and political accountability were at best vague, and at worst non-existent.

Although the weaknesses of London's governance system in this period were manifest, this period also witnessed some important progressive changes. Positive examples of partnership working at regional, sub-regional and local levels brought a wider range of actors with a wider base of expertise into the regeneration process, and developed new forms of co-operation

Table 1.1: A Chronology of London's Governance, 1986-2001

1986	Abolition of the Greater London Council (GLC), replacement with London Planning Advisory Committee (LPAC)
1990	Creation of Training and Enterprise Councils (TECs) (seven across London in 2000)
1994	Business Links set up to support small and medium size enterprises with between 10-200 employees
1994	Objective 2 status for the East London Lee Valley sub-region
1994	Government Office for London formed as one of 10 Regional Government Offices
1998 (May)	Referendum on London's Governance
1998	Formation of the London Development Partnership (LDP) forerunner to the LDA
1998	London Governance White Paper: A Mayor and Assembly for London
1999	Greater London Authority Act gained Royal Assent
2000	Publication of LDP's economic strategy *Building London's Economy*
2000 (4th May)	Ken Livingstone elected Mayor for London and 25 representatives elected to the London Assembly
2000 (15th June)	Michael Ward appointed as London Development Agency Chief Executive and George Barlow (Peabody Trust) as Chair
2000 (3rd July)	Formal establishment of the London Development Agency as the executive arm for London's economic regeneration activity
2001 (1st April)	London Business Link (LBL) (franchise of national Small Business Service) and local Learning and Skills Councils (LSCs) (five across London) officially came into operation

Source: Adapted from DETR (1998) London Governance White Paper

and ways of working across sectors. In response to the failures of past policies, an increasing emphasis on holistic approaches which drew together economic, social and environmental objectives, as well as a revived commitment towards community led regeneration, provided evidence of positive change in the latter parts of the 1990s.

London's New Economic Governance

In May 1998, following the publication of the government white paper 'A Mayor and Assembly for London', a referendum on the proposed new city-wide government structures was held. Despite a low turnout (34.6%), 72% of Londoners voted in favour of the proposals. In May 2000, the Mayor and members of the London Assembly[3] were duly elected. The key responsibilities of the Mayor and Assembly as set out in the GLA Act (1999) comprise transport, planning, economic development, environment, policing, fire and emergency planning, culture and health. Within the Authority there is a clear separation of powers between the Mayor who has an executive role and the Assembly which has a scrutiny role. The Mayor has responsibility for devising and co-ordinating strategies to tackle London wide issues[4], as well as a general power to do anything that will further the principal purposes of the GLA - to promote economic and social development and the improvement of the environment in Greater London. Two new executive bodies were set up to assist the GLA in formulating and delivering transport and economic development and regeneration strategies, respectively Transport for London (TfL) and the London Development Agency (LDA).

Within the GLA the Mayor has a key role in the development of economic development strategy. Not only does the Mayor have responsibility for producing an economic development and regeneration strategy, but also for producing strategies in other related areas, such as spatial development and transport, and ensuring that the preparation of these strategies is consistent and they involve wide consultation. The Mayor controls the new economic development body, the LDA, appointing the Chair and Board members and setting the administration budget. The Mayor is required to consult the Assembly in the preparation of strategies and the Assembly fulfils its scrutiny role on economic development issues via providing members (currently four) to serve on the LDA Board and via the cross party Economic Development Committee.

The London Development Agency

The LDA, which officially came into being on July 3rd 2000, has responsibility for modernising London's approach to economic development, by producing and implementing an economic development and regeneration strategy for London. It joins the eight existing Regional Development Agencies (RDAs) operating within England. Its powers are taken from the RDA Act (1998) as amended by the GLA Act (1999) (primarily Part V and Schedule 25). The statutory purposes of the LDA are to: further the economic development and regeneration of London; promote business efficiency, investment and competitiveness; promote employment; enhance and develop the skills of local people; and contribute to sustainable development.

Following the May 2000 election, the Mayor appointed the LDA's Chief Executive (Michael Ward), Chair (George Barlow of the Peabody Trust) and a 15 member board to lead the LDA. The Board is a hands on executive body and is required under legislation to be business led (currently nine members). The composition of the appointed Board illustrates a clear attempt by the Mayor to represent the diversity of London business, through the appointment of several leading businesswomen and black and Asian business leaders, and achieve a balance of other interests from across London[5].

The LDA currently has around 90 staff, but this is expected to rise to 120. Staffing comprises a mixture of existing employees from English Partnerships, the GOL as well as new recruits[6]. Funding for the LDA is routed via the Mayor and its budget results from a number of national funding programmes, Consequently the LDA has to operate within the existing financial constraints on economic development and regeneration in London. The annual budget is expected to be around £300 million, comprising mainly of funds formerly managed by the

London Region of English Partnerships and the SRB grant schemes previously administered by GOL.

The LDA is something of a hybrid animal; it has the same statutory objectives as the RDAs as set out in the 1998 RDA Act, but is different in certain key respects. Unlike the other RDAs, the LDA is a Mayoral agency, legally formed as a local authority, rather than a Non Departmental Public Body (NDPB), with the Mayor rather than the Minister for the Regions, approving the economic strategy and main policy instrument expenditure (Benneworth, 1999a). As the LDA has local authority status it is subject to the local government financial regime of 'best value' that applies to the London Borough Authorities. A further difference is that the Mayor's economic development strategy is scrutinised by elected members of the London Assembly. Thus through the role of the Mayor and Assembly there is an element of democratic accountability lacking in the other English RDAs. These differences have led to suggestions that the LDA will provide something of a test case for the future development of RDAs and regional government in England (Roberts, 1999; Harman, 1998).

A reality the LDA shares with other RDAs is that although they derive considerable power from the 1998 RDA Act to pursue aspects of economic development and regeneration, in practice the RDA role is limited by low levels of funding, a lack of control over key levers of economic development, and that other key elements (e.g. housing, transport, education) fall outside their jurisdiction (Tomaney, 1999; Jones, 1999; Mawson, 1999; Benneworth, 1999b, Hall & Nevin, 1999). RDAs do not control European Structural Funds (which remain under the control of the regional Government Office) and key institutions such as the Learning and Skills Councils (LSCs) and the Small Business Service (SBS) remain under the control of central government departments. There is also a total reliance on government funding streams with no statutory powers to raise their own additional finance. Despite confirmation of the lead role of the RDAs in economic development within the government's urban and rural white papers (DETR, 2000a & 2000b) and increased levels, and greater flexibility, of future funding, their capacity for autonomous action is heavily constrained. Given these resource constraints, the LDA will only be able to fulfil its brief to produce and implement an economic strategy for London through partnership working; leading and co-ordinating a diverse network of actors and agencies operating across sectors and at different scales.

Other institutions: Local Learning and Skills Councils and London Business Link

Alongside processes of political devolution, major changes in the delivery of small business support and post-16 education and training by the DTI and DfEE respectively, have created further important changes in the institutional framework for economic development within London. As part of the Labour government's policy to reform post-16 education and training (excluding higher education) the Learning and Skills Council was created to strategically develop, plan, fund and manage post-16 education and training provision in England (DfEE, 1999). At the sub-national level these services are delivered via 45 new Local Learning and Skills Councils which replaced the existing Training and Enterprise Councils and started operation on 1st April, 2001. In London there are 5 local LSCs (Central, North, South, East and West) which are intended to respond to the skills and learning needs of local labour markets and communities. Given the centrality of the skills and education agenda for the development of the London economy the five local LSCs are key institutions. The manner in which the LSCs co-ordinate activity with each other (and indeed with adjacent LSCs outside of the London area) as well as with other economic development agencies, will be highly significant to the overall strategic development of the skills and education agenda within London.

As part of their attempts to build an 'enterprise society' the Labour government launched the Small Business Service (SBS) in April 2000 to provide a single organisation in government dedicated to helping small firms and representing them in government. A principal objective of the SBS is to simplify and improve the quality and coherence of support to small firms. To achieve this a major rationalisation of the pre-existing 81 Business Link's (BLs)[7] took place and a new network of 45 BLs became effective from 1st April 2001. In London the SBS granted one franchise to London Business Link (LBL) which replaced the nine pre-existing Business Links. However there are five sub-regional offices of the LBL co-terminus with the five local LSC boundaries, thus reinforcing the potential importance of these five sub-regions in the future. In the publication of their draft strategy the LBL (2001) outlined a pan-London start-up strategy for small business and emphasised the broader remit for business assistance promoted by the SBS generally (i.e. to encourage and support entrepreneurship in all sections of society, for example across all ethnic groups, women etc.).

Structure of the Book

The development of this new institutional framework within London raises many questions concerning how these new institutions will develop and how they will interact with each other and the dense network of pre-existing actors and agencies. Can the new governance system deliver the co-ordinated and strategic pan-London economic development policies that have so obviously been lacking in recent years? Whilst it is clear that current changes provide new opportunities to achieve greater integration and co-ordination of policies and agencies, it is equally evident that they also provide many new opportunities for opposition and contestation.

The rest of this book seeks to explore these issues by considering the nature of the governance challenges that London currently faces with regard to economic development and regeneration, and what changes are needed to address them. In chapter two Gordon sets out the economic basis of London's competitive position. As part of the strongest economic region in the UK, the London economy presents unique governance challenges. Its sheer size, diversity, complexity and integration into the wider regional, national and international economy make it difficult to know just what is going on. Hence governance systems require a high level of sophistication. London's strong competitive basis means that unlike many regions the fundamental issue is not that of economic dynamism per se, but of ensuring continued economic dynamism on a long term basis and in a manner that benefits currently marginalised peoples and places.

The following three chapters (Newman, Clark, Thornley) analyse city-region governance within the international context and the issues this raises with respect to current changes in London. Newman (chapter three) draws from recent European experiences to argue that despite the apparently strong functional arguments that a new global economic era requires new city-region institutional forms, in reality these forms remain underdeveloped. Newman identifies a number of reasons why the creation of new institutions or greater co-operation between existing ones proceeds slowly; the difficulties in finding functional institutions acceptable to the multiplicity of existing institutions; ongoing intra-regional competition for public and private resources; differing local/regional traditions and political cultures; and the political opposition of local government.

Clark (chapter four) takes as his starting point the types of economic development issues faced by large global cities as a basis for considering the economic regeneration capabilities of the GLA and LDA from a comparative international perspective. He argues that global cities face distinct economic challenges and hence need a different 'toolbox' of economic development measures and governance forms to respond effectively. Comparison with other world cities leads him to conclude that Mayors and their development agencies elsewhere generally have more autonomy, power and greater financial and fiscal freedom; a fact which will clearly limit the capacity for intervention of the GLA and LDA, and will require them to operate closely with other stakeholders and institutions.

Thornley (chapter five) focuses on the issue of how the political and policy agendas of the GLA and LDA will be set and how co-ordination between institutions will operate in practice. By using the experience of city marketing in Sydney and Singapore as a starting point, he argues that agenda setting will be a political exercise based on power. However, the lack of clarity of existing legislation, the vague Third Way rhetoric which suggests diverse interests can be reconciled, and the complex networked nature of governance, all mean that there remains considerable uncertainty about how in practice the political agenda will be set in London, and whether it will be any more transparent and accountable than in the past.

The chapters by Sorenson, Bailey and Colenutt focus explicitly on the nature of the LDA and the challenges of partnership working within London. Sorenson (chapter six) takes the experiences of the London Development Partnership (LDP) (the forerunner to the LDA) to outline issues relating to the nature of the LDA and the economic challenges it faces. He points to the test the LDA faces in creating a strategic vision and developing an agency with an appropriate staff base and organisational culture, whilst operating with central government departments that continue to militate against joined-up working. Bailey (chapter seven) focuses on the legacy of partnership working in London and how the newly created institutions will interact with the existing institutional framework to develop a more strategic approach. Partnership working is entering a new period that promotes a strategic approach at city, regional, sub-regional and local levels via the creation of RDAs. Yet this new phase raises many questions, not least concerning the ability to develop an inclusive vision and strategy that is transparent and responsive to sub-regional needs, yet does not constrain economically dynamic sectors and effective service providers.

In focusing on the role of the London Boroughs (LBs), Colenutt (chapter eight) argues that the real needs of the LBs are likely to be overlooked by the new government of London. The continuing marginalisation and suspicion of local authorities by central government remains a major constraint upon delivering effective regeneration and service delivery and it remains unclear how the new governance structures will be able to improve this situation. He argues a more radical agenda is required that directs resources into front line services in targeted neighbourhoods and champions more community based approaches. In the absence of this type of agenda from the GLA and LDA, he is fearful of a split between LBs operating at the 'sharp end with local communities, and pan-London institutions operating at the regional level, with limited interaction between the two.

The chapters by MacGregor, Gidoomal, and Benneworth and Charles, pick up on the implications of current changes with regard to particular issues. MacGregor (chapter nine) discusses how in response to issues of poverty and social exclusion a new form of urban governance is emerging based on partnership and community involvement. Drawing on the results of a survey of urban leaders in London she identifies a range of beneficial recent innovations but also a continuing disjuncture between business led and people based approaches. Whilst an emerging emphasis on longer term community based strategies is to be welcomed, there remain dangers of unequal partners and communities being asked to take on tasks previously done by paid professionals. Gidoomal (chapter ten) focused on the issue of ethnic business as a huge and largely untapped resource in London. Despite increasing awareness of ethnic business there remains much to be done by the LDA and SBS to take forward the ethnic minority business agenda, and to make full use of London's ethnic diversity as a major foundation of its economic development strategy.

The role of Higher Education (HE) within London's governance system is explored by Benneworth and Charles in chapter eleven. The HE Sector has no clearly defined role within the GLA yet given the importance of education and learning to the London economy and the increasing organisation of the HE sector and their awareness of regional agendas, growing engagement between the universities and the GLA appears certain. How this relationship develops will be important given that the universities are one of London's major assets as well as being important economic, social and environmental players who potentially have a key role to play in delivering the regeneration agenda. The concluding chapter draws together the range of issues raised by the contributors and identifies the major governance challenges which London's newly emerging governance system faces in the field of economic development and regeneration.

Notes

[1] In the immediate aftermath of abolition 'strategic guidance' for London's planning was transferred to the Department of the Environment (DoE), with the 33 local authorities (including the Corporation of London) being limited to input through the London Planning Advisory Committee (LPAC).

[2] The London Pride Partnership published the *London Pride Prospectus* in 1995; an attempt to set out a vision for London for the 21sr century. The partnership consisted of the Association of London Authorities (ALA), the Confederation of British Industry (London Region), Corporation of London, London Boroughs Association (LBA), London Chamber of Commerce and Industry (LCCI), London First, London Planning Advisory Committee (LPAC), London's Training and Enterprise Councils, London Voluntary Service Council (LVSC) and Westminster City Council.

[3] The London Assembly consists of 25 elected members, 14 representing specific constituencies and a further 11 London members drawn from proportional party list voting

[4] The eight strategy documents the Mayor is required to produce include: transport, economic development and regeneration, air quality, noise, waste, biodiversity, spatial development and culture.

[5] The one notable exception in this respect is the failure to appoint anyone from the HE/FE sector. In recognition of this, representatives of the HE and FE sector have been granted 'observer' status on the Board.

[6] Unlike the other English regions where Government Office staff working in the SRB area transferred *en masse*, the majority of these GOL staff opted not to transfer into the LDA.

[7] Business Links provide information, advice and access to experts on all issues related to the running of a small and medium size enterprise.

References

Bailey, N. (1997) Competitiveness, partnership - and democracy? Putting the "local" back into London government, *Local Economy*, vol.12, no.3, pp.205-218.

Benneworth, P. (1999a) London Development Agency – the forgotten giant? Approaches to the establishment of the LDA and lessons for the English regional project, *Newsletter of the Regional Studies Association*, no.224, pp.11-21, December.

Benneworth P. (1999b) If this is the solution, then what was the problem? RDAs, the democratic deficit and 'joined-up thinking' in the English regions. Paper presented at *New Regional Strategies: Devolution, RDAs and Regional Chambers, Regional Studies Association*, London 26th November.

Benington, J. and Harvey, J. (1998) 'Multi-level, multi-nodal and multi-national governance'. In G. Stoker (ed) *The New Management of Local Governance: Audit of an Era of Change*, London, Macmillan.

Cooke, P. and Morgan, K. (1998) *The Associational Economy: Firms, Regions and Innovation*, Oxford, Oxford University Press.

Confederation of British Industry (CBI) (1997) *Regions for Business: Improving Policy Design and Delivery*, London, CBI.

Department of Education and Employment (DfEE) (1999) *Learning to Succeed*, DfEE, London.

Department of Environment, Transport and Regions (DETR) (1997) *New Leadership for London: The Government's Proposals for a Greater London Authority*, Cmnd 3724, London, HMSO.

Department of Environment, Transport and Regions (DETR) (1998) *London Governance the White Paper: A Mayor and Assembly for London, Department of the Environment Transport and the Regions*, London, London, DETR.

Department of Environment, Transport and Regions (DETR) (2000a) *Our Towns and Cities: The Future*, London, DETR.

Department of Environment, Transport and Regions (DETR) (2000b) *Our Countryside: The Future*, London, DETR.

Hall S. and Nevin B. (1999) 'Continuity and change: a review of English regeneration policy in the 1990s', *Regional Studies*, vol.33, no.5, pp.477-481.

Hambleton R. and Sweeting D. (1999) 'Restructuring our decision making', *Planning*, 12th November, pp.16-17.

Harman Sir J. (1998) 'Regional Development Agencies: not the final frontier, *Local Economy*, 13, pp.194-197.

Hebbert, M. (1995) 'Unfinished business: the remaking of London government, 1985-95', *Policy and Politics*, vol.23, no.4, pp.347-358.

Jones, M. (1999) 'The regional state and economic regulation: regional regeneration or political mobilisation? Paper presented at the *Sixth International Conference of Regional Studies Association*, 18-21 September 1999, University of the Basque Country, Spain.

Krugman, P. (1991) *Geography and Trade*, Cambridge MA, MIT Press.

Labour Party (1995) *A Choice for England*, London, Labour Party.

Lloyd P. and Meegan R. (1996) 'Contested governance: European exposure in the English regions', *European Planning Studies*, vol.4, no.1, pp.75-97.

London Business Link (2001) *Making London the Best Place to do Business*, London, LBL.

London Pride Partnership (1995) *London Pride Prospectus*, London, LPP.

Mawson J. (1997) 'New Labour and the English Regions: a missed opportunity?' *Local Economy*, November, pp.194-203.

Mawson, J. (1999) 'Devolution - the English Regions and the challenge of regional governance', in M. del P. Gardner, S. Hardy and A. Pike (eds) *New Regional Strategies: Devolution, RDAs and Regional Chambers,* London, Regional Studies Association, pp.4-10

Newman, P. (1995) 'London Pride', *Local Economy*, vol.10, pp.117-123.

Newman, P. (2000) 'Changing patterns of regional governance in the EU', *Urban Studies*, vol.37, no.5-6, pp.895-908.

Newman, P. & Thornley, A. (1997) 'Fragmentation and centralisation in the governance of London: influencing the urban policy and planning agenda'. *Urban Studies*, vol.34, no.7, pp.967-988.

North D. and Baldock R. (2000) 'From crisis manager to strategic partner: the changing role of four London Boroughs in economic regeneration', Town Planning Review, vol.71, no.4, pp.435-454.

Regional Policy Commission (RPC) (1996) *Renewing the Regions: Strategies for Regional Economic Development*, Sheffield, Sheffield Hallam University.

Roberts P. (1999) 'From here to eternity: future prospects for the RDAs and regional governance' in M. del P. Gardner, S. Hardy and A. Pike (eds) *New Regional Strategies: Devolution, RDAs and Regional Chambers*, London, Regional Studies Association, pp.107-113.

Robson B., Parkinson M. and Robinson F. (1994) *Assessing the Impact of Urban Policy*, London HMSO.

Scott, A.J. (1998) *Regions and the World Economy*, Oxford, Oxford University Press

Stewart M (1994) 'Between Whitehall and town hall: the realignment of urban regeneration policy in England', *Policy and Politics*, vol.22, no.2, pp.133-145.

Storper, M. (1997) *The Regional World: Territorial Development in a Global Economy*, New York, Guildford Press.

Tomaney J, (1999) 'The case for English regional government', in M. Del P. Gardner, S. Hardy and A. Pike (eds) *New Regional Strategies: Devolution, RDAs and Regional Chambers*, London, Regional Studies Association, pp.100-106.

Chapter 2

Unpacking 'Competitiveness' as a Governance Issue for London?

IAN GORDON

Urban Competitiveness

For many good (and some less good) reasons economic competitiveness, social cohesion and environmental sustainability have become key concerns for cities over the past decade, and central to expectations of the new London governance system (ALG, 1998; LDP, 2000). This represents a very demanding agenda, since each of these aims stands for a bundle of concerns - loosely identifiable as economic, social and environmental - and since there is no necessary complementarity between them. In the current jargon, addressing these clearly requires 'joined-up' thinking, but what cannot be afforded is a 'short-circuited' thinking that focuses on particular, convenient dimensions of competitiveness, cohesion and sustainability and *assumes* that a particular policy stance will secure each of these. There is, for example, little reason to believe that boosting the competitive position of London businesses will of itself do anything much to reduce the appalling concentrations of unemployment remaining in eastern parts of inner London - reflecting the weak competitive position that many groups of residents occupy within the regional labour market.

Even in terms of economic competitiveness there are great ambiguities because cities compete (increasingly) in many different ways for mobile investment and human resources, public grants and projects and a larger share in the markets for goods and services. The last of these seems the most fundamental, though the economist Paul Krugman (1996) has argued that, since it is actually firms that compete in these markets, it is a great

23

mistake to think about cities (or nations) as competing with each other. This may seem a pedantic point, given the evidence from Michael Porter's (1990) work that particular city-regions confer distinct kinds of competitive advantage on firms based there, and Krugman's (1995) own strong argument that modest shifts in competitive advantage can have major long term effects through urban scale economies. Indeed Krugman himself (1995) recognises that 'an intellectually respectable case' *can* be made for public policy intervention in such situations - but he is deeply sceptical about almost all particular cases, since these tend to be disguised forms of special pleading for very particular interests.

In relation to the London economy, two major problems in coming to grips with what the city's competitiveness means, and how it can appropriately be advanced, relate to its extraordinary scale, diversity and complexity, and functional interdependence with the surrounding region. These present both intellectual problems in comprehending how the competitiveness of the system as a whole is to be understood and advanced, and political difficulties in securing a balanced representation of the range of stakeholders who need to contribute to the making of a competitiveness strategy.   In this situation, an understandable temptation is to over-simplify the situation, focusing on one or a few of the more coherent complexes of activities (and interests) as basic to the whole, and on the challenges posed by the most readily identifiable sets of rivals. A danger of the 'global city' concept is that it can lend itself to a reductionist approach of this kind, with the health of a few core 'global' activities in the central area seen as the key to the city's long term prosperity. A healthier interpretation of 'globalness' would be to see the highest international standards as the benchmark against which all London's activities have to compete, with quality (of products, assets and Londoners' lives) rather than quantity as the criterion of success.

The question under consideration in this book is how, and how far, new governance structures for London can contribute to success in these terms. As a starting point for examination of this issue, this chapter considers two sides of the context in terms of first, the key characteristics of the London economy, and second, the typical problems with the pursuit of economic competitiveness by European cities. A concluding section offers some initial suggestions as to how these problems might be mitigated as the new London institutions are developed.

Change, Markets and Competition in London

The London economy has been through 40 years or so of extraordinary change, and this continues to be the case. A conspicuous element in this change has been a great shrinkage of employment in those sectors offering predominantly manual jobs. But the story has been one of massive restructuring, not of failure, and - in contrast to Regional Development Agencies (RDAs) in the old industrial regions - the core task of the new London Development Agency (LDA) is not one of plugging gaps in an economy devastated by deindustrialisation. To say this is not to deny that in terms of poverty and unemployment substantial parts of inner London have problems as intense as those of northern cities, when comparisons are made at the level of local authority districts or parliamentary constituencies. Because of London's much greater scale as an economic unit, however, these comparisons can be very misleading. A 10% unemployment rate within parts of London has a very different significance from a similar rate of unemployment recorded for Merseyside as a whole. In the first case the problem is that many local people face severe difficulty in competing for a stock of jobs in the city which is more or less adequate; in the second case, however, the problem is mostly that there are too few jobs to go round. In both cities there is a great deal still to be done about improving the competitive position of disadvantaged groups within the labour market, as well as a need for RDAs to create assets which enhance business competitiveness. But in the London case there is not the same need to bring in activities or investment to secure employment, which implies a rather different, and more sophisticated, role for the LDA.

In fact, London represents the spatial core of the economically strongest region in the UK (if not of the EU).

Nowadays, however, this region extends a long way beyond London - as in Peter Hall's (1989) notion of a Greater South East, stretching from Cambridge to Dorset - with outer areas contributing substantially to its strength. Finding appropriate indicators of competitiveness is not easy, but it is significant not only that overall productivity is highest in Greater London, but that most of the British activities for which Porter finds evidence of competitive advantage are particularly concentrated in this region. The recent EU Community Innovation Survey also demonstrates the superiority of this region over other parts of the British economy in terms of rates of product innovation, although in this case real strength seems to lie entirely outside Greater London (Simmie and Sennett, 1999).

Four key aspects to the region's competitive potential are:

1. A uniquely strong combination of agglomeration economies, including a very flexible labour market, accessible in varying degrees from inner and outer parts of the region.
2. A very large pool of advanced skills, based on a combination of the attraction of highly qualified people from across the UK (and abroad) and the human capital enhancing characteristics of work and interaction possibilities in the city.
3. A concentration of key decision-makers, both in the public and private sectors, to whom many businesses and other organisations require face-to-face access.
4. Very strong international links, in terms of personal and information flows, coupled with particular expertise in interpreting international intelligence.

Crucially, these are all among the kinds of asset whose value has been enhanced by the type of economic environment which has been evolving over the past couple of decades, implying the potential for a substantial boosting of the region's competitive position, unless impeded by other shortcomings.

Among possible obstacles, the most basic is the space constraint on development, particularly within the continuously urbanised core of Greater London - although planning policies make it an issue in much of the hinterland as well. Its main effect has been to inhibit substantial employment growth, especially in activities needing low-rise forms of development. With income and productivity growth generating demands for lower densities of occupation, general economic success in the city has thus been accompanied by a trend towards shrinking levels of employment and population since the early 1960s. For population this trend has been halted by the concentration in London of recent waves of international immigration, but for employment it continued through the period of increasing 'global' activity within the city (Gordon, 1999).

One consequence of the combination of space constraints, and continuing economic success, is the fact that London is a relatively expensive location from which to operate (both by UK and international standards), with high rents, house prices, and (consequently) both high wage and service costs. This serves to 'squeeze out' routinisable functions and activities not requiring frequent face to face contact with other London based actors - both through actual moves and through frustration of growth aspirations among firms which remain. A very important implication is that the city has to compete on quality, originality, responsiveness and productivity, since London businesses will often start from a cost disadvantage.

As far as activity within London is concerned an important consideration is that many of the key agglomeration economies are readily accessible from centres in 'ROSEland' (i.e. the Rest of the South East). This is particularly true in the 'western crescent' (running from Hertfordshire through Berkshire and Surrey to West Sussex), where Heathrow access is better than for much of London, and which actually houses much of the region's highly skilled labour force (e.g. in business services and IT). It is in these outer areas that London's strength as a centre for innovation is now most conspicuously displayed, with Greater London only exhibiting 'average' rates of product innovation, perhaps because its comparative advantage is greater in functions such as 'deal-making'.

Since the early 1980s, another important characteristic of the region has been a high degree of instability, in employment levels (as well as in rents, house prices, and development activity). This contrasts with the relatively greater stability (compared with more industrial regions) experienced in the previous half century, and seems likely to be a continuing reality. Reasons for the shift include the combination of financial deregulation (including that of the mortgage market) with the shift to a post-industrial economy (in which regional consumption levels become a more significant factor), and continuing speculation about the impact of new developments on London's status as an international centre. This instability has real consequences, particularly in the labour market, but also makes it much harder to gauge the meaning of short/medium term economic developments.

In retrospect it is easy to identify the boom and bust of the late 1980s/early 1990s as two sides of the same coin, but it is as yet unclear whether the last seven years of growth in London employment represents the first part of a similar cycle, or the beginning of a more settled trend (see Figure 2.1). The temptation now, as in the 1980s is to read it in the latter way, as an indicator of real success, but this temptation to optimism is a part of boom phenomenon - with the current hyping of the creative sectors paralleling the 1980s exaggeration of the role of world city activities (Gordon, 1999). In formulating economic development strategies, the new London authorities will need to maintain a degree of detachment from such speculation, concentrating rather on factors relevant to the longer term trends of development in the city.

The other clear and important message of past trends in the London economy involves the very limited extent to which employment trends within London, particularly in the service sectors, actually impinge on the level of unemployment and associated poverty within the city (and particularly in the inner east boroughs). The scale of this problem varies strongly with the state of the wider South Eastern economy. Essentially, however, it reflects a weak competitive position within this regional labour market of a number of population groups who happen (for housing market reasons) to be residentially concentrated in these areas (Buck et al., 1997).

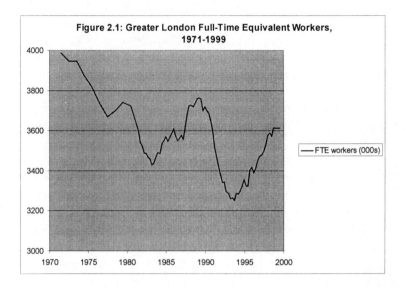

Figure 2.1: Greater London Full-Time Equivalent Workers, 1971-1999

The opening up of a substantial gap in unemployment rates between Greater London and its regional hinterland over the past twenty years (including some of the 1980s boom years) marks not a relatively poor employment trend within London (even for manual jobs), but a progressive marginalisation of the most vulnerable during years of general labour market slack. Reversing this is not simple (though New Deal initiatives should actually help), but the key point to appreciate in relation to economic development strategies is the negative one, that employment expansion within London is more or less irrelevant for this task (i.e. neither necessary nor sufficient).

Predictable Biases in the Promotion of Territorial Competition

In contrast to the United States, promotion of local economic activity is not one of the traditional responsibilities of local governments in Europe, but economic competitiveness has increasingly emerged as a policy concern at local or regional level since the 1980s. One reason for this was the emergence of high levels of urban unemployment during the recessions and the perceived need to take some action to find a new economic base in areas experiencing severe deindustrialisation. Other more structural factors included recognition that qualitative characteristics of particular places were becoming more important as competitive factors, and the potential exposure of major cities to more competition from centres in other countries following completion of the Single European Market (Cheshire and Gordon, 1995).

In London's case the last of these factors was clearly one of the stimuli to the series of studies of its competitive strengths and limitations vis-à-vis other pretenders to 'global city' status launched in the early 1990s (including CLD, 1991; CRP, 1995; and LDP et al, 1996). Up until now it has not had the institutional capacity to follow through on any of these studies. The loss of a strategic authority for London just as private sector interest in global city activities and locations took off does seem particularly 'unfortunate', although it is notable that it was the 'substitute' strategic planners and standard bearers for London (LPAC and the City Corporation) which recognised this issue, rather than the GLC itself. However there have been widespread difficulties in many other European cities in responding to these new challenges, not just in London, even though it was unique in the destruction of its metropolitan authority.

The basis of the general problem is that launching of a new, unprogrammed bottom-up form of economic intervention requires a substantial local coalition of interests to promote it, which is hard to achieve. This is particularly the case in large and diverse metropolitan areas lacking a strong sense of regional (or nationalist) identity - unless strong leadership is available (e.g. from central government). Where such a coalition can be built, it is almost inevitably based on the active involvement of a rather small group of quite particular interests, which are potentially major beneficiaries. More generally, and perhaps especially where the degree of effective commitment is weak, there is a strong pressure for visible activity with demonstrable immediate outputs, in order to meet symbolic needs and ensure survival of the agencies/programmes involved (Cheshire and Gordon, 1996).

The effects of this characteristic institutional and competitive weakness of territorial competition initiatives in most places is not only to limit its scope, but also to encourage a number of understandable, but damaging biases in the sorts of activity which are pursued. In particular, these include:

1. An over-emphasis on inward investment, which is neither the major contributory factor to area's above/below average growth performance - a role played by in situ growth of establishments - nor usually a good indicator of what would assist local businesses to realise their potential (Cheshire and Gordon, 1998).
2. Types of promotional activity which are either purely wasteful (like most forms of image promotion) or generate compensating losses in other areas (often within the same region and/or with a comparable need for additional jobs and investment).
3. A tendency to mimicry of currently fashionable forms of urban development (e.g. multi-purpose CBD or waterfront renewal projects) or targeted activities - allowing mobile businesses to play one place off against another, thus reaping all the gains from competition – rather than exploiting comparative advantage to create unique selling features from which the place can profit (Cheshire and Gordon, 1998).
4. Focusing on potential benefits to the *place* without considering how far, and how, these benefits can be attached to local *people*, particularly those in most need. For example in terms of the likelihood that new jobs actually increase employment rates among residents; in the worst scenarios where new short-lived branch plants attract in migrants to fill most of the jobs, who stay on after those jobs have gone, employment rates can actually be reduced by inward investment.

In each case, the point is not simply that there are more and less effective ways of pursuing local competitive strategies, to which attention needs to be paid. Rather it is that structural factors inhibiting the development of strong and representative bodies pressing for a balanced development of the urban economy are liable to encourage policies with negative outcomes for the majority of interests outside the active coalition. This danger is particularly salient in a city such as London with a large and diverse economy (now spreading well beyond Greater London itself) and a weak tradition of metropolitan leadership.

The Governance Task in London

The message of this paper is two-sided. On the one hand, there is clearly a need for strong London-wide institutions to advance the competitive position of its economy, in the interests both of the nation and of London residents (including the economically disadvantaged). On the other, there are many difficulties and temptations to be overcome in ensuring that strategies and sets of actions justified in these terms actually make a positive contribution to the long-term interests of those who are supposed to benefit – with a real possibility of being counter-productive in these terms. This is the challenge for the new London institutions.

In part this is an analytic challenge, of moving beyond simplistic ideas and indicators of what is to be counted as competitive success. The body of past work on developments in the London economy, briefly summarised here, is enough to show, both that such success is quite compatible with a shrinkage in the volume of employment within the city itself, *and* that neither success nor quantitative expansion (within London) can be counted on, of themselves, to relieve the problems of economically deprived groups in the city.

The focus has to be on understanding more clearly two issues. First, the ways in which public policy can enable businesses to add value to their activities in London, focusing on quality rather than quantity. Second, how the benefits of competitive success can be extended more widely across groups, areas and sectors in the city. But it is also a political/institutional challenge, to find ways of pursuing economic advantage which avoid the characteristic biases of territorial competition, for example by:

- Focusing on avoiding/relieving unnecessary constraints on growth of existing and potentially dynamic businesses (including space constraints).
- Identifying and addressing cases of real market failure (e.g. education for intermediate skills, or training for the hospitality industries).
- Collaborating rather than competing with the two RDAs with formal responsibility for other parts of the functional London region (e.g. in relation to the western and eastern corridors).
- Facilitating development of distinctive London assets not easily replicated elsewhere, whether in other leading European centres or in the secondary centres which are likely to become increasingly effective competitors for various specialised parts of the city's service business.
- Engaging expertise from a range of key productive sectors in the development of strategic policies and initiatives, not just inputs from the property and 'regeneration' industries.

References

Association of London Government (1998) *The London Study: The Future of the City*, London, ALG.

Buck, N., Crookston M., Gordon I.R. and Hall P.G. (1997) *A Socio-Economic Assessment of London*, report by Llewelyn Davies and Partners for the London Study, London, ALG.

Cheshire, P.C. and Gordon, I.R. (eds) (1995) *Territorial Competition in an Integrating Europe*, Aldershot, Avebury.

Cheshire, P.C. and Gordon, I.R. (1996) 'Territorial competition and the predictability of collective (in)action', *International Journal of Urban and Regional Research*, vol.20, no.3, pp.383-399.

Cheshire, P.C. and Gordon, I.R. (1998) 'Territorial competition: some lessons for policy', *Annals of Regional Science*, vol.32, pp.321-346.

City Research Project (1995) *The Competitive Position of London's Financial Services: Final Report*, London, Corporation of London.

Coopers and Lybrand Deloitte (1991) *London: World City Moving into the 21st Century*, London, HMSO.

Gordon, I.R. (1999) 'London and the South East' in M. Breheny (ed) *The People: Where Will They Work?*, London, Town and Country Planning Association, pp.169-186.

Hall, P.G. (1989) *London 2001*, London, Allen and Unwin.

Krugman, P.R. (1995) *Development, Geography and Economic Theory*, Cambridge, MA, MIT Press.

Krugman, P.R. (1996) *Pop Internationalism*, Cambridge, MA: MIT Press.

Llewelyn Davies Planning, UCL Bartlett School of Planning and Comedia (1996) *Four World Cities: A Comparative Study of London, Paris, New York and Tokyo*, London, Llewelyn Davies.

London Development Partnership (2000) *Building London's Economy: A Strategy For The Mayor And The London Development Agency*, London, LDP.

Porter, M.E. (1970) *The Competitive Advantage of Nations*, New York, Free Press.

Simmie, J. and Sennett, J. (1999) 'Innovative clusters: global or local linkages?', *National Institute Economic Review*, 170, pp.87-98.

Chapter 3

Reforming Metropolitan Regions - European Models?

PETER NEWMAN

Introduction

The reform of London government can be understood on a number of levels. At a generalised level of explanation, globalisation and international city competition seem to demand a visible and vocal mayor to speak up for London. Another level of explanation would refer to the need to solve the problem of managing a dominant metropolitan economy in the relatively small state of England. Yet another explanation would refer to Europeanisation of governance and the introduction, following the recently created government regional offices, of a European style, regional level of government. More domestic explanations refer to New Labour's constitutional reform project and the continuing evolution of central-local government conflicts over government of the capital city.

This chapter starts by looking at the value of more generalised levels of explanation and at the European context for metropolitan reform. It soon becomes clear however when examining other European experiences, that changing metropolitan governance is better understood not as an inevitable product of global city competition, but as the outcome of the interaction of local pressures with national political and constitutional contexts. These outcomes in many cities seem to represent at best partial and temporary resolution of problems of governing metropolitan areas.

Functional Regional Government

In both Europe and the US scholars have identified economic regionalisation as a powerful organising force in a global economy. Economic geographers identify clusters of regions with dynamic urban cores (Scott 1998). At the same time political scientists point to the 'denationalisation' of space (Brenner, 1999, p.435) as nation states seek to promote their cities and regions in a competitive environment. Both types of analysis argue that institutional change is needed to match government institutions to the new economic spaces of a global economy. In Brenner's terms there are 'institutional prerequisites' (p.440) of economically competitive regions. Scott (1998) makes a similar case for new necessary governance institutions to manage regionalised economies. Institutions and policies need to change. Barnes and Ledebur (1997) argue that it is the regional and not national level where the new economy has to be managed.

A more cautious line is taken by Jessop (2000) arguing that the nation state has lost its leading role but that, as yet, no one level of government takes precedence. The difficulty for the simpler, arguments of functional necessity is that it is hard to point to cases of new effective institutions emerging in the right places. Lefèvre's review of metropolitan government in Europe (1998) finds few exemplary cases and Le Galès and Lequesne (1998) conclude that there is no consistent picture of regional government across Europe.

It is nonetheless the idea of global pressures which pushes forward the agenda of regional and metropolitan reform. In 1999 the Organisation for Economic Co-operation and Development (OECD) published a draft set of principles of metropolitan government. The authors argued, following the economic geographers, that, as metropolitan areas play an increasingly important role in the global economy, the way in which they are governed has become crucial to their ability to grasp economic opportunities and resolve questions of social cohesion and environmental sustainability (OECD, 1999). Many cities had outdated government structures and the OECD identified widespread concerns about the transparency and accountability of decision making. There is thus an international agenda of metropolitan reform, and we might expect to find cities moving along similar paths.

It can also be argued that the history of European scale regional funding has both encouraged a regionalisation of government and a Europeanisation of institutional forms. Certainly the search for European grants has been a strong factor in creating alliances between public and private sector actors. In the case of the UK it is not however clear whether the Europeanisation of governance has benefited regional, national or European institutions (Martin, 1998). In the UK as in other unitary states, regional funding remains in the control of national government. Other states have devolved more responsibilities to regions. Relationships between different scales of government have undoubtedly become more complex and some attempts have been made to schematise the uncertain emerging structures of European governance. Governance can be seen as 'multi-level' (Marks, 1993) or as a system of overlapping 'spheres' (Benington and Harvey, 1994) of authority. Thus it is by no means clear how new regional institutions fit into changing governance across Europe. Europe's city regions are managed by differing combinations of local, regional and national level institutions. New institutions at city region level may be a necessity in a global economy and the desired objective of supranational bodies, but actual experiences show a diversity of forms of governance across Europe.

European City Regions

National context obviously has an impact on the emergence of new governance institutions. Some states have attempted to change the boundaries and functions of formal institutions of regional government. However proposals for regional reform in Amsterdam and Rotterdam failed in referendums. Constitutional reform in Italy has been slow with uneven responses. The Portuguese rejected regionalised government in 1998. Actual forms depend on national context but also in interaction of national and sub national institutions and the extent to which new regional identities can transcend economic and political constraints. The alternative to comprehensive new institutions is to foster intergovernmental co-operation. In France national legislation has encouraged a variety of forms of intercommunal co-operation. Comprehensive metropolitan government was set up in most large cities in the 1960s through the indirectly elected *Communautés Urbaines* which share multiple functions, including planning and development, and in some cases sharing tax revenues between communes. Recent legislation favours more co-operation through *communautés de villes* and *communautés d'agglomération* in the largest urban areas. Such nationally enforced intraregional co-operation is the exception and reflects the particular compromises between local, regional and republication politics in France. In other countries voluntary intraregional and city-suburban co-operation is rare.

However, the potential benefits of city regional scale government seem to be well understood. In the US the 'new regionalism' focuses on the economic and fiscal, and sometimes environmental benefits of city suburban co-operation (see Swanstrom, 1996 and Savitch and Vogel, 1996). In reviewing international trends for the OECD Heinz (1998) suggests three main reasons for intergovernmental co-operation. First is the functional dispersal of urban activities. These activities spread beyond central city boundaries and their functional links require institutional and policy co-ordination. The second reason is, as we have discussed, the regionalisation of funding and in particular the encouragement given to intraregional co-operation by European funding programmes. Such funding may however only encourage short-term co-operation Thirdly fragmented authority across functional regions may work against competitiveness. There are therefore good reasons why new city regional institutions should be created through co-operation. But there seem to be several strong forces which hamper such ambitions.

Finding functional institutions acceptable to the multiplicity of interests in large urban areas can be a complex process. The recent history of Frankfurt and its region exemplifies this. Concerned about increasing inter regional competition the chambers of commerce and large municipalities pressed for structural reforms and the replacement of the UVF (*Umlandverband Frankfurt*) by a new regional union, which would have a range of powers with its own resources and measures for equalising local government finances. Alternative proposals emerged and it became clear that some preferred a Regionalkries Rhien-Main which would operate as a single tier, and between there were differing ideas about objectives, functions and boundaries (Heinz, 1996). A further point emerging from the Frankfurt case was the identification of regional consciousness in the local population as a crucial factor. Without a sufficiently strong vision of the benefits of co-operation institutional reform fails or is very slow.

A second reason why co-operation fails to develop is competition. The French *Communautés Urbaines* worked where they had been imposed on communes by national government. In areas with looser regional arrangements, such as the Paris region, intercommunal competition tends to undermine co-operation. For example in the western suburbs of Paris a group of communes joined in a strategic planning syndicate (such single purpose institutions are common in a highly fragmented local government system) to plan economic and population growth. However, the communes chose a weak institutional form and local mayors remain engaged in dogged competition over the location of new commercial development (Boyer, Decoster and Newman, 1999).

Political competition can also get in the way of co-operation. The Région Urbaine de Lyon proposed in the late 1980s was the product of the political ambition of the mayor of Lyon. The fact that this functionally defined urban region accounted for 80% of the GDP of the existing Rhone-Alpes region drew the understandable opposition of the President of the elected regional council (Bardet and Jouve, 1998).

A third set of factors which work against co-operation are those embedded in tradition and political culture. In Lisbon for example there are some signs of interest in new forms of metropolitan governance. But Seixas (1999) argues there are limits to such initiatives. Traditions of clientelism prepare few local mayors for new forms of governance. At metropolitan level Lisbon is made up of 18 municipalities with each mayor capable of blocking co-operation. The mayors tend to prefer informal arrangements and there have been no meetings of the strategic council of the city of Lisbon in recent years because it is politically irrelevant.

Another powerful set of factors arise from the practical opposition of local governments fearful of losing authority or mindful of local financial difficulties. The Berlin city region offers a good example of such forces. In the Berlin region incentives to co-operate look particularly strong and recognition of interdependencies led both Berlin and Brandenburg governments to support a formal merger. However, the referendum on merging the two Länder in 1996 failed to win popular support in Brandenburg. Brandenburg was particularly wary of being subsumed by a dominant city, but both Länder were aware of their financial problems and unconvinced about the benefits of co-operation.

Nevertheless there were strong grounds for co-operation. Both Berlin and the Land Brandenburg have financial problems. Since the stetting up of the two Land governments at the beginning of the 1990s population and business have moved across formal regional boundaries. The functional integration between the two formal regions can also be seen in the issue of airport development, the location of new distribution centres, and out of town shopping development. Some limited response has been made to these obvious interdependencies in the fields of economic development, hospital and university planning, and security. A joint planning department and joint regional plan for an area extending about 20km from Berlin's borders has been in place since 1998. However, the regional plan only reflects existing local plans and the intended joint economic development agency has not been set up. Co-operation is confined to those less controversial areas where both Länder stand to win, for example areas like tourism policy, joint applications for European and Federal funding and international marketing. However when it comes to decisions on the location of new development within the city region - business, retail parks and housing - co-operation disappears.

Some innovative sub regional planning has emerged in various sectors crossing the border between the two Länder. Such processes have been facilitated by external consultants and involve municipalities and districts of Berlin rather than the city itself. Such relatively weak forms of co-operation produce strategic plans but do not tackle fundamental issues of housing or economic development. There are other informal co-operation mechanisms, around the development of environmental strategies for example, but all of these attempts to build regional co-operation from the bottom up depend for resources on the Länd governments at which level political support for co-operation is weak. The involvement of the City of Berlin in the affairs of local governments bordering the city would be politically unacceptable to Brandenburg politicians. The local governments either side of the regional border are reluctant collaborators. The reasons for the lack of co-operation between local governments are obvious when the financial and political circumstances are examined. Within both Länder there are falling revenues, high unemployment and high costs associated with modernisation. These financial pressures on local political leaders get in the way of co-operation. For many political leaders local decision making is new and not to be given up to higher levels, when the benefits of co-operation are much less tangible than immediate financial gains and votes at the next election.

Thus in a city region where functional imperatives point clearly to the benefits of regional co-operation, existing structures shape actual outcomes and the political and financial realities of local governments determine the speed and degree of co-operation. The Berlin case points to the determining role of constitutional factors, formal institutions of government and the local cultural factors which in this case create distrust of higher level government. Similar sets of factors are highlighted in accounting for the greatly contrasting experience of metropolitan co-operation in Bologna (Jouve and Lefèvre, 1999). The history and culture of collectivism in the city region made possible co-operation in a new '*Accordo per la Cittá Metropolitana*'.

Conclusions

Intraregional co-operation in most city regions is underdeveloped. Yet this arena of regional co-operation is identified as important both by academics and policy makers. Understanding why effective city regional government is the exception needs to focus on both local political factors and national constitutional contexts.

Where co-operation does occur it is around policies where each side sees positive gains. Regional co-operation in Berlin and elsewhere is most likely where the expectation is 'win-win'. Such narrow thinking may however be missing opportunities. It may be possible to show that regional development is not a zero-sum game but building support for such views is a long term process. A political problem facing regions at whatever scale they are conceived is how to create and sustain legitimacy for new institutions and policies. Intraregional co-operation only seems to work when benefits are visible and tangible to all parties. The legitimacy of new institutions depends on their ability to break out of short term electoral politics and how well they can establish consensus around wider regional goals. European experience suggests that city regional co-operation is often problematic and comprehensive regional institutions rare. At city region level formal solutions, redrawing boundaries and setting up new regional governments, tend not to work for long.

The new institutions of London government respond to popular demands for a voice for London, but also expose other regional governance problems. New relations with neighbouring authorities in the functional urban region have yet to be worked out as do new co-operative arrangements of economic governance between Boroughs, LDA and training agencies. In a European context such incomplete city regional reform is unexceptional.

References

Bardet, F. and Jouve, B. (1998) 'Defining a new territory as a means of building a political stronghold: the invention of the Region Urbaine de Lyon', *Space and Polity*, 2 pp.127-144.

Barnes, W. and Ledebur, L. (1998) *The New Regional Economies*, Thousand Oaks, Ca.: Sage.

Benington, J. and Harvey, J. (1994) 'Spheres or tiers; the significance of trans-national local authority networks', in P. Dunleavy and J. Stanyer (eds) *Contemporary Political Studies*, Belfast, Political Studies Association, pp.943-961

Boyer, J-C., Decoster, E., Newman P. (1999) 'Les politiques de revitalisation des aires d'ancienne industrie à Londres et en Ile-De-France', *Cahier No 11*, Paris, Insitut Français D'urbanisme.

Brenner, N (1999) 'Globalisation as reterritorialisation: the re-scaling of urban governance in the European Union', *Urban Studies*, vol.36, pp.431-451.

Heinz, W. (1996) *Intraregional Co-operation in Metropolitan Area: Frankfurt and the Rhine-Main Area*, Cologne, Deutsches Institut Für Urbanistik.

Heinz, W. (1998) *Co-operative Approaches Between Core Cities and their Environs*, Occasional Papers, Berlin, Deutsches Institut Für Urbanistik.

Jessop, B. (2000) The crisis of the national spatio-temporal fix and the tendential ecological dominance of globalizing capitalism, *International Journal of Urban and Regional Research*, vol.24, no.2, pp.323-360.

Jouve, B. and Lefèvre C (1999) 'La cité métropolitaine de Bologne', in Jouve, B and Lefèvre, C. (eds) *Villes Metropoles*, Paris, Anthropos.

Le Galès, P., Lequesne, C. (eds) (1998) *Regions In Europe*, London, Routledge.

Lefèvre, C. (1998) Metropolitan government and governance in western countries: a critical review, *International Journal of Urban and Regional Research*, vol.22, pp.9-25.

Marks, G. (1993) 'Structural policy and multi-level governance in the EC', in A. Cafruny and G. Rosenthal (eds) *The State of the European Community: Volume 2*, Harlow, Longman.

Martin, S. (1998) 'EU programmes and local governance in the UK, *European Urban and Regional Studies*, vol.5, pp.237-248.

OECD (1999) *Draft Principles of Metropolitan Governance*, Paris, OECD.

Savitch, H.V. and Vogel R. (1996) *Regional Politics*, Thousand Oaks, Ca.: Sage.

Scott, A. (1998) *Regions and the World Economy*, Oxford, Oxford University Press.

Seixas, J. (1999) *The Future of Governance in Lisbon City Region: Expected Urban Politics for the XXIst Century* Mimeo.

Swanstrom, T. (1996) 'Ideas matter: reflections on the new regionalism, *Cityscape*, vol.2, pp.5-21.

Chapter 4

The International Context: Considering the Economic Regeneration Capabilities of the GLA and LDA

GREG CLARK

Introduction

At this early stage in their development it remains difficult to assess what the Greater London Authority (GLA) and London Development Agency (LDA) might achieve in terms of economic development and regeneration. However, one interesting starting point for developing what will undoubtedly be an ongoing debate, is via comparison of their potential vis-à-vis other global cities. In this chapter I will examine the economic regeneration capabilities of the GLA and LDA within an international context. In so doing I will be working to a number of assumptions:

- The economic development and regeneration roles of the new London arrangements should be viewed as potentially pertaining to the whole new GLA apparatus, not just the LDA (e.g. the roles of transport, policing, culture and tourism, sustainable development and the spatial development framework will be central to economic regeneration).

- The economic development and regeneration roles of the GLA and LDA will be but a part of London's overall apparatus. Central Government (e.g. the Government Office for London (GOL) and various departments/agencies such as the Department of Trade and Industry (DTI) and English Partnerships (EP)), the Boroughs, the European Union (EU), the Small Business Service (SBS), Learning & Skills Councils (LSCs), business groupings, Greater London

Enterprise (GLE) and many others, will also be playing important roles (e.g. the London SBS will have around 400 employees whilst the LDA will have only around 120).

- The economic development and regeneration agenda of a global city (like London) is unlikely to be the same as many of the other regions of the UK, and comparison with the English, Scottish, or Welsh Regional Development Agency (RDA) activities may be of limited value. More useful might be comparisons with other major cities - New York, Paris, Berlin, and Toronto are those that I will consider in this chapter.

- The new London arrangements are not static, but evolutionary. It is valid to begin the debate about how the arrangements could be strengthened and improved immediately whilst still being supportive of what has been started.

Whither Mayors and Development Agencies?

For many years the UK has been borrowing public policy initiatives from the USA and Europe. In the realm of urban policy in particular, American models have provided the impetus for many of the innovative approaches which have enabled the UK to be a leading exponent of urban renewal across Europe. In turn, European models of regional development, social partnership, local administration, and civic infrastructure have been developed and adapted to the UK as a focus for municipal modernisation and devolution.

Thus, Urban Programmes, the Urban Development Corporations, Training and Enterprise Councils (TECs) and public/private partnerships all had their origins in the USA. Simultaneously, Regional Innovation Strategies, 'Guarantee Systems', and R&D Grants have been largely European imports. More latterly, Welfare to Work, in-work tax credits, Inner City Enterprise Markets, Community Reinvestment, Small Business

Investment Companies and Business Improvement Districts have received significant attention as the current crop of US initiatives which we are seeking to 'borrow' from across the pond. Moreover, as the Urban White Paper published in November 2000 reveals, our politicians are more excited than previously about the achievements in Rotterdam, Barcelona, and Stockholm, and are keen to borrow their City Development Corporations, Urban Regeneration Companies, Neighbourhood Management, and design standards. Some ministers are even expressing interest in Regional Development Banks and other sub-national investment institutions.

The most significant 'urban initiative' that the UK Government has so far sought to transfer from the USA and Europe is the directly-elected City Mayor. With London as the pathfinder, and several other British cities waiting eagerly to follow, enormous excitement has greeted this development, linked as it is to the Government's programme of constitutional renewal, progressive devolution, and the modernisation of local government

It is anticipated that London's mayor will help London's economy, and work to foster the competitiveness of its businesses and locations, applying a visionary metropolitan leadership to important issues like transport, policing, skills, employment, regeneration, investment, tourism, culture, and planning. But the notion that an additional administrative tier can make an economy more successful needs some substantiation. It is not usually argued by business leaders that they need more government in order to be more competitive!

If the new London Mayor and those of other British Cities (that hope to follow) are to succeed in helping our urban economies to regenerate, they must also understand that they will have to work with a very different tool box from their US and EU counterparts.

Mayors and Leadership of Economic Development and Regeneration

As macro-economic policies in the developed nations converge through the globalisation of markets and economic management (e.g. World Trade Organisation (WTO), EU, North American Free Trade Agreement (NAFTA) there is perceived to be increasingly less to choose between countries, other than the cost of production (reflected principally in exchange rates), on the many issues that influence business and investment. In place of national variations, the emphasis has shifted down to regional, especially metropolitan, tiers where significant advantages might now be gained by pursuing distinctive strategies that can offer businesses a better platform for success, and a higher return on investment. Metropolitan leaders, especially city mayors, can now, more than latterly, make a regional economic difference if they get it right.

For those concerned with Britain's urban areas, city mayors should therefore be good news. Few mayors win elections, or enter office, without promising to bring or create new jobs, retain important local firms, improve skills and tackle unemployment, dereliction, and inactivity. It goes with the office of mayor that the city economy is a primary concern, and one that he or she is expected to address with great vigour. The mayor's mandate, derived from being directly elected as the 'first citizen' of his/her city, requires that he/she develop a broad coalition around a vision for the city economy; bring private, civic and public leaders to the table, and create a single economic development 'system' from amongst otherwise disparate efforts. The mayor consults, spells out a strategy, and then uses every power or lever that can be mustered to persuade everyone to back it. This could create an important cultural change in the UK. Rather than focussing municipal energies on gaining more public grants through the various challenge funds, city mayors can remind everyone that the real goal is to help generate investment and build capacity and enterprise. This could help unravel the perverse incentives to demonstrate poverty in order to win grants, rather than demonstrating productivity, in order to win new investment.

Economic development and regeneration can therefore become a core dimension of the mayor's over-arching objectives. Mayors will want to see how housing, culture and leisure strategies contribute to economic objectives, and will expect their teachers and police officers to be knowledgeable about the city's economic opportunities and future aspirations. Without ever legislating for it, economic regeneration can quickly become 'a statutory duty' of all municipal employees.

City mayors across the developed world share some of the same economic development tools: control of city planning, police, sanitation and public housing, combined with an influential role in transport, airports, education, tourism, infrastructure and culture. Many mayors will raise up to 50% or more of their own balance sheet from directly levied taxes, and will be free to discount or increase taxes in universal or targeted ways for both specific or general purposes (e.g. to encourage enterprise and investment in certain locations). Most will have some powers to raise investment capital against anticipated taxes and other revenues, ownership of a wide-ranging income earning property portfolio, and the freedom to lend, borrow, invest, save, sell assets (and keep the receipts) and abate taxes to create an incentive structure that bites.

The majority will also have a dedicated economic development corporation or agency. Often run as a public/private partnership, but reporting to the mayor, they can have extensive executive powers, and can 'do deals' with private sector partners on land, investment, or R&D. The financing arrangements of such agencies/corporations are usually within a separate envelope that puts them outside of the Public Sector Borrowing Requirement (PSBR), and have a status as regulated financial intermediaries within regional and national capital markets. The typical tool box of most city mayors is full of instruments that few economic regeneration professionals in the UK have ever been free to use.

Whilst many of the economic tools may be similar, the strategies and methods are not always so. Economic development and regeneration will often mean different things to mayors in vastly varying cities. For Mayor Mikkelson in Copenhagen the priority has been new infrastructure links across national borders through bridge and tunnel to Malmo, as a means to open up a new bigger regional market for labour and supplies. For Mayor Frank Sartor the Olympic Games provided the platform to re-position Sydney as the economic capital of Oceania.

Mayor Goldsmith in Indianapolis decided that the privatisation of many city services was the best way to stimulate growth in smaller supplier firms with export potential. Mayor Diepgen in Berlin sees the re-location of the Bundestag as the spur for a new media and services industries, and Mayor Giuliani knows that lower taxes and lower crime will do more for the New York City economy than any local development programmes might. For Mayor Penelas in Miami it is the combination of continental location with racial and linguistic diversity that creates the scope for a strategy to become the economic capital of Latin America.

The Global City Context

Over the past two decades, several new models of regional economic development programmes have emerged in the context of global economic and political restructuring. Such regional development programmes often aim to plan and finance new infrastructures, and to bring together efforts to attract and retain companies to the regions, alongside initiatives to stimulate the creation of new firms locally. Linked to these efforts are initiatives to improve innovation and productivity in existing firms, and facilitate the benefits of clustering amongst local firms and their supply/distribution chains. These are then complemented by efforts to improve the skills and employability of the local labour force, and the recycling of under-used, disused and derelict (brownfield) land to create new locations for economic activity. The most frequent objective of such activity is to increase regional Gross Domestic Product (GDP); the same task given by the British Deputy Prime Minister to the new English RDAs.

The range and variety of ingredients of a typical regional development programme are indeed very wide, and emphasis will vary from one type of region to another. For example, in the UK post-industrial regions supported by EU regional development programmes, there has recently been a strong emphasis on upgrading technology and innovative capacity.

In several states of the USA there have been concerted efforts to build cluster based strategies that will support the growth of high value-added manufacturing or other 'export' industries, such as movie production. In the transition regions of Central and Eastern Europe more emphasis has been placed on the processes of reform and privatisation, and the building of a responsive commercial environment for a mixed economy in terms of legal and financial regulations and services (e.g. finance, technology, real estate). Indeed, it can be argued that new regional development models have grown up to suit the range of regional contexts that now exist.

In this light it is worth asking what the regional development context of a city like London (or New York, Paris, Berlin, Toronto, Los Angeles) is? How can we categorise such cities in economic development policy terms at this stage in their evolution? What are the typical economic development challenges of a large city that is at the very top of the global urban hierarchy? Are these challenges different from those in other regions and are they well understood by state and national governments? Do they require a broadly similar, or very different, approach from those regions with which they share a national government?

One way to begin an answer to such questions is to seek to define some of the most exceptional or unique aspects of the challenges such cities face. Some of the main considerations would include:

Size and complexity

These cities are extremely large and dense by comparison with other places. They have larger GDPs and populations than most medium sized countries. London has more people than Ireland,

Wales, or Scotland; New York City's economy is greater than that of Mexico. The cities have extra-ordinarily diverse economies, with leading industries (e.g. finance, tourism, creative industries, business services, aviation) that serve local, national, and global markets equally successfully. They command complex technological infrastructures and have very wide ranging governmental relationships. They occupy a unique place in the 'command and control' structures of the world economy and bear testament to the maxim that the global economy is made and produced in such cities. This very size and complexity means that there is less obvious scope to develop and manage their economies through local efforts.

Leading sectors and traditional industries

The prominent sectors and the leading corporate actors which are the economic engines of cities like London, New York, Paris, and others scarcely require government funded economic development assistance to ensure their competitiveness. However, the leading sectors co-exist alongside more traditional industries (manufacturing, public services, local retail, print, ports/docks, etc.) that are in longer term processes of transition. The extent to which these traditional industries are able to share resources, and price structures (especially for land, labour, infrastructure and services) with the leading edge globally traded sectors is a challenge for economic development policy. Put more simply, the apparent economics of business in these traditional industries suggests they should be located in quite different places.

This involves difficult questions of prioritisation. On the one hand, some of the traditional industries may well be able to underpin the diversification of roles, jobs, and incomes across the city economy, and, on the other hand, there is little room for public policy initiatives to underpin 'declining' industries. Prudent judgement is required about which sectors to support and how to calibrate that intervention.

Wealth and poverty

These cities are also the sites of an extraordinary range of wealth and incomes. London, Paris and New York feature near the top in global figures for regional GDP. However, these cities also demonstrate very high proportions of unemployment, poverty, and urban deprivation. The extent to which these cities can use their own wealth to tackle their own poverty therefore becomes a major focus of concern. Mechanisms to harness re-investment potential and to spread the benefits are therefore all important. This suggests that it could be critical for global cities to be empowered to use their natural advantages and resources to address their own critical problems, and to exercise the potential for the city-region to become a self-correcting mechanism. This is only largely possible where the city has control of its budget and assets and is able to promote much longer term investment/return equations than a 'higher tier' government might allow. If the global city's regional investment programme is totally controlled by national public finance strategies (driven by national political and economic cycles and fiscal goals) it is unlikely to optimise re-investment in those regions (e.g. global city regions) from which the higher levels of taxation come.

Old geography, new economy

There are important spatial dimensions to the economic development challenges of these cities. Their relatively long histories, and pre-eminence in the industrial era, means that their townscapes are often mature and settled. They have established central business districts and town centres, inner and outer suburbs, industrial corridors, transport hubs and terminuses, and well defined sports, entertainment and retail locations. There is very rarely any land that is not already fully developed, legally protected, caught in a site assembly problem, or being deliberately 'land-banked' for future profiteering off other anticipated investments.

These cities are also often land-locked (either by water in the case of New York and Toronto, or by the Green Belt in the case of London, or by older boundaries in the case of Berlin) resulting in the requirement to recycle urban land effectively and to be able to re-organise the local economic geography to support new growth, industries, and firms or new housing and community development. However, in the context of very fragmented land ownership patterns, and costly 'sunk investments' in infrastructure and utilities, and 'sunk liabilities' in contaminated sites and derelict buildings, this recycling of land is far from simple and affordable in all cases. Poorer families and communities are often much less mobile than companies and are often less able to respond positively to such changes of use.

The complex calculus of generating new urban locations which are attractive and accessible to their intended users is one that requires the co-ordination of a very unwieldy mesh of owners, tenants, regulators/planners, financiers, service providers, and other functionaries. This co-ordination does not come easily, and is rarely in the hands of a single development agency or regional government, as it might be elsewhere (in a 'greenfield' or post industrial location).

Cities and regions

An important additional aspect of the 'old geography/new economy' challenge in global cities like London is the city/region dynamic. The functional economic region for labour, investment, supply and distribution in most such cities is now well beyond the old municipal political boundaries, which have become frozen in time. The challenge is to try to develop *local* economic policies that have *regional* coherence so as to both minimise unhelpful intra-regional competition, and to avoid 'displacement' (where the impact of policies is merely to move an activity, job, or firm, from one part of the region to another with no net benefits). The difficulty of achieving this kind of regional coherence in economic development policies between cities and their outer suburbs, or outlying smaller cities and town, is acute - even more so in the fiscally empowered local governments of USA operating without regional governments, than in the regionally empowered governments of some parts of Europe, and the centrally financed municipalities of the UK.

High cost/high value

The higher costs of cities at the top of the global urban hierarchy pose an additional challenge. There is a strong link between the risks and returns of being a primary location of higher value added industries like finance and business & professional services, and the general cost base of doing business or living in such a city. An obvious manifestation of this issue comes in the real estate market, where the price of commercial or residential property in cities like Paris, London, and New York remains stubbornly high and rising at levels well above the average direct growth levels of the urban economy itself. One impact of this is to make it hard for these cities to easily support 'entry level' activity like accommodation for small and medium sized enterprises (SMEs), or affordable housing for new workers. Without specific local and regional initiatives the real estate market will not easily deliver these lower yielding property uses, and the city will lose an important source of new jobs and new dwellings.

Fiscal surplus/investment deficits

Cities that house the higher order functions described earlier are important to the treasuries and exchequers of their state and national governments. Independent calculations for both London and New York suggest that they are both contributing a net surplus of around £20,000,000 ($30,000,000) per year to higher tiers of government. Both cities also however have very significant investment deficits in transport, education, infrastructure, regeneration and other amenities. In many cases, national and state governments also place strict limits on the amounts of investment the cities can make and on the debt they can issue (London's boroughs and GLA are particularly circumscribed) through budget capping and regulation.

The challenges for economic development policy here are manifold. It is important not to substitute small-scale 'economic development programmes' in the place of the larger scale investments in public services and infrastructure that will be necessary to render the economic development policies achievable. It is also important not to make short term 'economic development deals' with individual firms at the expense of longer term investments in whole industries and locations.

Open labour markets and unemployment

The very openness of the labour markets creates unusual problems and opportunities for these cities. Los Angeles, Paris, London and New York attract talented and enterprising people from across the world to come and participate in their labour markets, but they also maintain very high levels of unemployment amongst their indigenous populations. Some of these mobile workers are the 'captains of industry' or the young mobile post-graduates of every nationality who seek the top jobs in the high value sectors. Others are the migrants, refugees, and immigrants who are seeking an entry into the labour force at whatever level is possible.

An even larger and more substantial secondary work force includes the one million or so commuters that each city welcomes each day and loses each night. These cities also house huge contingent labour forces in the shape of returners, students and 'double jobbers' (for example the many waiter/actors, nurse/nannies, teacher/cab drivers, that one sees) many of whom would prefer more permanent employment that provides better benefits and conditions. Some functions in the cities encourage the casualisation of work, creating a large 'contingent' labour force (increasingly operating within an informal economy). Concentrations of activity in cleaning, security, hospitality, maintenance, construction, and retail may encourage this more.

Higher than average levels of unemployment in these global cities provides an economic development challenge which is clear. There is increasingly no automatic link between the creation of jobs in the city economy and the reduction in the numbers of local people who are officially unemployed. There are simply so many other people competing with the unemployed for the jobs that are created, and the unemployed are often less competitive in their skills base and employability. Economic development policies have to address the competitiveness of the unemployed in the labour market and (simultaneously) the mechanisms for accessing jobs and incomes.

Mobility and volatility

Berlin, Toronto, New York and London are all cities with higher than average levels of volatility and mobility in their small business base, in their residential populations, and in their labour forces. Policies that seek to aid individuals and firms may well find that they achieve their aims only to see the individual or firm leave the city or neighbourhood in which they are based. Evaluations of urban regeneration in London have sought to understand why unemployment in not lower in certain poor neighbourhoods after many years of public investment in the people there.

The answer is that the investments have indeed been successful in enabling numbers of people to find work, only to see them move to a better neighbourhood as soon as they can afford to do so and to be replaced by the new influx, or next generation, of the unemployed. Initiatives to start new companies often see the most successful ones leave the city after they have established a network of customers and suppliers.

The economic development policy challenge here is to find ways of spreading the benefits and costs of the economic development programmes more evenly, and at the same time, to capture and concentrate the benefits of successful economic development in the places whether it can make the biggest difference.

The Economic Development and Regeneration Agenda for Global Cities

This overview of economic development challenges from cities like London suggests a distinctive economic development agenda that will not be well met by partial policies that are not joined-up, nor by national policies that are not refined to the global city context. Economic development programmes that are largely defined and shaped by national priorities, budgets, formulas, and fiscal capacities are unlikely to be effective at delivering the investment required to become a sustainable global city. London has common economic development challenges with Paris, New York and the others but has a rather different tool-box.

A key lesson from all of this seems to be that, given the constraints on achieving anything in a 'piece-meal' manner, it is going to be essential to seek integration and co-ordination between a very wide range of services, inputs and initiatives. At the very least it is necessary to co-ordinate:

- Income with expenditure and investment in the city economy.
- City with region, central business districts (CBDs) with neighbourhoods, inner with outer city.
- Housing policies with education and transport (and economic development strategies).
- Business, public, and community leadership in all its forms.
- Jobs creation with measures to tackle unemployment.
- Small businesses development with urban revitalisation.
- Cluster and sector strategies with technology and innovation programmes.
- Inward Investment marketing and promotion with business retention.
- Spatial planning and transportation with the re-development of derelict and brownfield sites.
- Community economic development and area revitalisation programmes.

Not only do we need to see the co-ordination of these activities one with another, but we need economic development policies to have a real relationship with much wider efforts to develop and govern the city and its region. For global cities like London, local economic development policies are not going to work effectively without:

- The integration of economic development policies into the wider governance system (local, city-wide, regional, national, etc.).
- The co-ordination of economic development strategies and wider public service offerings (land-use planning, policing, education, housing, transport).
- More direct mechanisms to deliver investment to economic development priorities from fiscal and financial policies and governmental revenues.
- Better calibration of the role of economic development policies and investment vis-à-vis market based provision from banks, real estate developers, utility companies, and the leading companies in each sector.

Global cities are not the only places that need economic development policies, but given their relative strength in headline measures of GDP and related indices, a different kind of economic development framework is required. Growth alone is not delivering the benefits widely enough, and there is no strong evidence that growth alone will *spread* rather than *concentrate* rewards. The kind of growth does matter, and the diversity of opportunity it can create and the mechanisms it affords for participation are critically important.

The Mayor's Economic Development Dilemmas

Economic development and regeneration can give the mayor of a global city bad dreams. There are some intrinsic problems in this component of the job description. Economic time and political time vary widely, it takes a decade or two to achieve local economic development outcomes, whilst most mayors have only four years to prove themselves. Economic geography and political geography are also out of synch; successful strategies will rarely benefit the 'city' alone, with wider regional benefits often more likely than improvements in the poorest neighbourhoods. Competition is rife, and always changing, and there are hard decisions to be taken about the risks and returns of exposing the municipal balance sheet to economic gambles that might not come off. Given these pressures, some mayors have been known to shift emphasis towards the highly visible/touchable mega-projects like new sports stadia, exhibition centres, and theme parks. Most now look for a combination of longer term 'wise investments' (which could ensure their legacy) with 'quick wins' that court attention and media praise (which might aid re-election).

Assessing the Mayor's Economic Development Tool-box

The question for London, and for the other British cities that will hope to follow, is how to create a sufficient economic development tool-box for the new British city mayors. Our context remains one of fragmented urban governance (where central government funded agencies are still not yet well connected to local government and civic initiative), watertight central control of public finances, and very constrained powers of local government action. London's mayor will have to succeed in helping London's economy without many of the powers available elsewhere. Our cities are not 'blank sheets' or greenfield sites, and the agenda for urban economic regeneration requires that concerted action between many different parts of the public sector, private and civic sector be a realistic objective of our new mayoral class.

To have the best chance of economic development success, our European and American counterparts show us that a Mayor needs to have:

- A city boundary that is wide enough to approximate nearly to a functional economy without leaving important suburbs or industrials districts outside.
- Some 'regional reach' that enables cohesive economic action between city, suburbs, and outlying areas.
- Direct control of key powers to plan land-use and infrastructure, housing and education, police and transport, and the authority to make them work together.
- Influence over other important public sector bodies in health, higher education and culture.
- Ability to 're-write the contract' between the city and its business community through shaping and focussing the municipal tax system.
- Ability to bring forward necessary investment through borrowing against assets and anticipated revenues, and the ability to be in partnership with financiers sharing risks and returns to the benefit of the city as a whole.
- Capability to create new executive agencies that can operate in the margins between public sector services and mature market economies.
- Ability to create long term programmes that can be stewarded by civic partners to get away from the cyclical reversals of political seasons.

One way to start to assess whether we have a new city government with economic development and regeneration capacity is to try to define how the GLA (and the LDA more precisely) measure up on some of these factors against the benchmark of some other cities. No scientific model exists, so what is presented below is an embryo for a way of looking at these issues. It is intended to be illustrative of certain important issues rather than comprehensive. Essentially, it is suggested that we can 'score' the GLA and LDA on some broad measures that might indicate economic development and regeneration capability. The measures used are as follows:

For the GLA:

- How well does the boundary fit with a functional metropolitan economy?
- How well do the broad powers allow it to engage directly with the full range of economic development and regeneration activity?
- How far does it control the services that are important to the city economy?
- How far does it have economic development tools which are fit for purpose?
- How far can it use its own fiscal strategies and initiatives to engage business partnership or investment?
- How far can it innovate financially to bring forward new forms of investment and financing which benefit the city economy?

For each of these six measures there is notional score (out of 10) allocated and comparative score for each of New York, Paris, Toronto, and Berlin. The 'scores' are based on a working knowledge of each city, but are not the product of a precisely constructed formula or calculation. They are, to that extent, anecdotal and will be open to question and improvement, perhaps even to a fuller project.

Table 4.1 The Economic Development Capability of the GLA in an International Perspective

	GLA	NYC	Paris	Toronto	Berlin
Boundary	7	6	4	5	7
Powers	5	8	8	6	8
Services	7	8	6	6	8
Tools	4	8	4	4	6
Fiscal	1	6	5	5	8
Financial	2	8	8	6	8

Comparing the powers of the new London Mayor and Government on these themes, against mayors and city governments in New York, Toronto, Paris, and Berlin, can be a disappointing endeavour (see Table 4.1). The London Mayor's economic development capabilities look reasonable on the boundary question (though not as good as Berlin) and comparatively weak on almost all of the others, with very low scores on all aspects of tax and finance, and many aspects of service management and cohesion. New York and Berlin are vastly more powerful mayoralties, with more that twice as much power as the London mayor will have, and great abilities to engage in economic development activity. Paris is weak on the boundary issue but has some significant strengths in finance and taxation, and shares some of London's weaknesses in service co-ordination, and Toronto's very average scores on most counts never dip down to London's lows.

The general picture that this comparison reveals is of a comparatively weak Greater London Authority, especially when compared to New York City Government or to the Berlin State Senate. Perhaps this is unsurprising, both New York and Berlin live within systems of government that provide for quite exceptional levels of autonomy at the city level. The point is rather to show that London has some quite stark deficiencies on the financial and fiscal side and there must be some doubt as to how a city-wide economic strategy which may be heavily dependent on central government transfer payments can properly achieve its aims.

With over 95% of the anticipated budget coming in formularised transfer payments from central government, London's mayor has insufficient autonomy. To a large extent, central government may continue to be the major initiator in economic development terms, and whilst few would argue that is right for macro-economic management, many will question what a mayor is for when such little flexibility exists for an urban economic strategy that has any teeth. There appears to be little scope to create a London Regeneration Block Grant (bringing the myriad funding regimes together in a flexible way) or establish a

London Investment Bank in the way that Mayors of other cities might seek to do.

For the LDA the questions are:

- How far does the strategy provide the co-ordination function for the city as a whole?
- How far does it manage, or have responsibility for, the important economic development and regeneration programmes?
- How far can it build up its own asset base and revenue streams to engage in re-investment?
- How far is it able to join-up different aspects of the public services and infrastructure to achieve economic development and regeneration goals?
- How far is it able to embrace the functional metropolitan region with its activities?
- How far can it create strategies and programmes which are long term and not overly subject to variations in public finances and political control?

Table 4.2 The LDA in an International Perspective

	LDA London	EDC NYC	PDA Paris	TEDCO Toronto	IBB Berlin
Strategy/Co-ordination	6	8	6	5	4
Management/ programmes	5	8	4	4	4
Asset/ Finance	3	10	4	8	10
Joined Up	4	8	5	2	6
Region	5	4	8	0	8
Time	4	4	6	5	8

The general picture that emerges from this comparison for the LDA is one of a broadly based capacity, but perhaps a lack of bite (see Table 4.2). In comparison with counterparts in Berlin, New York, Paris, and Toronto the LDA is stuck within an economic development and regeneration 'system' which could be too fragmented to allow for concerted action and might lack authority. This means that LDA success (unlike say the British Urban Development Corporations of the 1980s and 1990s) will be very highly dependent upon good working relationships with boroughs and others at the local level, and with central government and it's sponsored organisations (e.g. Small Business Service, Learning and Skills Councils, at the regional level).

Making London's Model Work

So, London's GLA and LDA will have a very different set of instruments from the American and European global cities to bring to the service of the London economy. Where they issue city investment bonds to modernise infrastructure, London's mayor may need specialist private fund managers outside the public finance envelope and PSBR. Where they abate taxes to achieve business retention, London's mayor may need to make hard cash available or reduce their costs in other ways (maybe working with utilities and landowners). Where, in the US and EU, they re-zone the city and compulsorily purchase sites to create new economic districts, London's mayor will have to persuade several boroughs to work together with the LDA to do it. London's approach will be 'contingent' rather than 'imperative'.

However, London's mayor will not have some of the challenges that American and European mayors must face. There will be no competitive tax reductions from the South East to tempt businesses away from London (although there maybe some London firms that are seen as desirable to poach and there may be other reasons to leave related to general pricing rather than tax). Many of London's finest cultural assets will continue to be financed from the national purse and the Lottery, and impossible dilemmas of budget virement between long term investments, such as education, and short term emergencies, such as snow-ploughing, will not exist in quite such dramatic ways!

All in all London's mayor is a new and unique type of post for the UK. London's leader is not the president of a regional council or chair of a metropolitan government, nor the typical 'big city mayor' of American or European cities. All mayors find that they control some of the tools for the job but not all of them. In each case the mayors of many famous cities must use the influence of the office to develop an agenda for the central business district, for the inner city, and for the suburbs and wider metropolitan area. Making this agenda sufficiently compelling to get all the stakeholders to join the effort is the task at hand, and whatever tools and resources are available must be used to that end.

The mayor of London will need to be an entrepreneur, gathering together through vision, influence, and persuasion the opportunities and resources required to do some new deals for the capital. The London mayor will need to be a tool-maker, using the London Development Agency to create a new set of economic development instruments out of the interplay of private enterprise, civic good will, public assets and commercial disciplines. The GLA and LDA will have to much more conscientiously orchestrate and manage their own 'supply chains' of companies and organisations that have some of the capabilities that city government might have elsewhere. For example, the core LDA with it's 100 or so staff and £300,000,000 budget will be augmented by the LDA 'suppliers', developers, banks, utilities, other asset/fund managers, as well as the public sector bodies that one can envisage. London's economic development and regeneration 'supply chain' will need to learn that there can be benefits of having a small strategic city-wide authority that needs to work with others to get things done.

No doubt we all watch with great enthusiasm and interest as things unfold. A fundamental judgement will be whether the distinctive aspects of London's arrangements turn out to be a strength or a weakness. How much financial and fiscal power will the UK Government eventually release to the capital? And will it be increased flexibility in *how* money is spent rather than *how much* is spent and *how it is raised* that comes first? The metropolitan/local split (in terms of services and functions) between the GLA and the Boroughs will be an important dimension in how the new approach evolves and many will see this relationship as offering some fundamental scope for further reform.

Chapter 5

Agenda-Setting in the GLA with Particular Reference to City Marketing and the Role of the LDA

ANDREW THORNLEY

Introduction

This chapter raises some questions about the agenda-setting process within the new London government arrangements. What will be the institutional mechanisms to draw together the varied economic, social and environmental aims of the new organisation? City marketing, one of the functions of the Greater London Authority (GLA) and the London Development Agency (LDA), will be used as an illustration of a potential influence on the establishment of priorities. How will the aims of this particular activity fit into the broader goals of the GLA? The experience of city marketing in Sydney and Singapore will be briefly outlined to raise some questions for the London case. It is suggested that at the end of the day the determination of the agenda remains a political exercise based upon power. It will be interesting to see how the GLA will mediate these political pressures. At this early stage in the GLA's development one can still only speculate over this, and in the final section of the paper some issues are raised concerning the future role of the LDA.

Globalisation, City Marketing and Politics

One of the key objectives of the LDA will be to enhance London's competitiveness. This naturally requires an understanding of the processes of globalisation and an exploration of London's role in the changing world economy. City

68

marketing seeks to ensure that a particular city is on the world's 'business map' and is attractive as a location for inward investment. In this sense city marketing can be viewed as emphasising a particular interpretation of economic globalisation. Held et al. (1999) have identified three main schools of thought that have evolved regarding globalisation. These are hyperglobalisers, sceptics and transformationalists. Hyperglobalisers, usually emanating from the business world and Management Schools, believe that global economic forces will dominate all activity and inevitably reduce the power of nation states. Sceptics claim that 'globalisation' is over-hyped as a new phenomena and is basically no different from the operation of international capital in the past. In contrast transformationalists see something different and significant in the globalisation process and believe that it will generate very new conditions. They also see the outcome of this new process, including the impact on the role of the state, as uncertain and open to influence.

A key issue is that these different reactions have different political connotations. From the hyperglobalisation viewpoint the role of politics is to ensure that a particular country or city responds directly to the imperative of the new global economy. In this way it will maximise the benefits to a particular locality. The concept of trickle down is applied to the global scale and city marketing is a central strategy. The political implications of the sceptic view is that as there is nothing particularly new about the situation the political response of the past is still appropriate, particularly the socialist approach. Transformationalists believe that major changes are taking place but that politics, if it also takes on new forms, can have importance in shaping the particular outcome of these changes.

As a context for looking at London it is worth briefly noting the reaction of the New Labour government to the globalisation process. In the campaign for the 1997 general election Blair stressed the need for Britain to respond to the forces of globalisation. For example he said, 'since it is inconceivable that the UK would want to withdraw unilaterally from the global market-place, we must instead adjust our policies to its existence' (Blair, 1996, p.86). This rather passive and responsive attitude would seem to place the government in the hyperglobalist camp. However since then we have witnessed the development of the 'Third Way' building upon the ideas of one of the transformationalists, Anthony Giddens (1994;1998). This seems to open the way to a more flexible political approach, although clearly rejecting what is regarded as the sceptic's 'out of touch' socialism.

How will the new approach in London reflect these different responses to globalisation? Will the city marketing imperatives dominate or will they be tempered by aims and objectives oriented to needs other than those of global business and finance? One way of exploring this will be through an analysis of the way in which the policy agenda is constructed and the priorities that result. Different interests will have different priorities and will seek to ensure that these are high on the agenda. The new structure of governance in the city will provide the framework within which these interests will have to operate and will influence the degree of power each set of interests can exert. One of the interesting issues to explore in relation to the establishment of the GLA will be whether the new structure of metropolitan government will make any changes to the previous interplay of interests which influenced the agenda setting process in the early 1990s (see Newman and Thornley, 1997). One approach would be to explore the way in which the different objectives of the GLA are pursued and co-ordinated[1]. Before outlining some ideas and questions in relation to such an exploration, two comparative examples of the city marketing approach will be introduced into the discussion.

City Marketing in Sydney and Singapore

Clearly there are major limitations in looking at only two cities and this exploration is used to simply raise some questions in relation to London. Sydney and Singapore are cities that have placed a lot of emphasis on developing their 'World City' role. They have adopted strong city marketing strategies. Both Sydney and Singapore also have political structures that have allowed the development of a metropolitan-wide strategy (although these structures differ from those of the GLA). They have, alongside their city marketing, established strategic plans for the whole city and it is therefore possible to see some of the implications of the interplay between city marketing and comprehensive city-wide plans. Questions can then be posed for the relationship between the city marketing function of the LDA and London's Spatial Development Strategy (SDS).

Sydney has established itself as the leading Australian city, with the best international air connections and largest financial business centre. It seeks to become a location for transnational corporations wanting to operate in the whole South East Asian region. In 1995 the State of New South Wales, responsible for the strategic planning of the city, produced a new metropolitan strategy that sought to be more flexible and promote Sydney as a regional business centre. It said, 'as we move into an age of more rapid change and diverse global influences, a metropolitan planning strategy needs to be dynamic' (Department of Planning, 1995, p.12). The following year the State commissioned a report assessing Sydney's strengths and weaknesses as a Global City (Searle, 1996) and the conclusions were incorporated into a revised strategy produced in 1997. However this was still not considered sufficient for some interests and in the same year a pressure group, called 'The Committee for Sydney', was set up led by business leaders. This group, which was supported by the State Premier, felt that a more focussed vision was needed to promote Sydney further as a World City so they commissioned consultants to prepare this.

Meanwhile in Singapore the government was reassessing the role of the city building on the advice of the business community. Since independence in 1965 the government, through the Economic Development Board, had taken a leading role in identifying an economic strategy that adjusted 'the Singapore economy to the niches and opportunities in global capitalism' (Chua, 1998, p.983). The Singapore government was able to use its power to orchestrate the implementation of such a strategy. In the 1980s it was decided to shift the emphasis away from manufacturing and make Singapore the hub of business and finance for the South East Asia region. Once the new economic agenda had been set then this was translated into land use and development terms by another arm of government, the Urban Redevelopment Authority. A new Concept Plan was prepared in 1991 which was a very direct and clear tool for the implementation of the new strategy to promote the city as a 'World City'. The plan states that its aim is to 'restructure the city for business'.

In both cities there was a very clear identification of the role of the city in relation to the forces of globalisation and an emphasis on promoting this role in a competitive environment. A suitable 'vision' was formulated with strong support from the local business community. This then had a very direct influence on the content of the strategic land use and development plans. London of course over the last decade has also been assessing its World City role and numerous reports have been produced. The London Pride Prospectus (LPP, 1995) might be regarded as a similar vision statement. However without a strategic authority there has been no opportunity to translate this directly into strategic planning terms. One of the questions is the degree to which the new Spatial Development Strategy (SDS) will act as a tool for the implementation of a city marketing strategy.

Another major theme that is evident from the examination of Sydney and Singapore concerns the means of ensuring the implementation of the strategic vision. The issue here is that pursuing a World City orientation results in the desire to implement certain kinds of development such as financial centres, new office locations, leisure and conference facilities, hotels, luxury retailing and restaurants. These developments often have no direct benefits to local residents. As Judd (1999) and others have noted they often lead to 'bubbles' of development that are divorced from the surrounding community. It is not surprising therefore that there is often local opposition to these developments. One of the features therefore of the city marketing strategy is that it is accompanied by various mechanisms to implement the strategy notwithstanding such opposition. In Singapore this is achieved by a strong central authority with very few opportunities for any expression of local feeling. In Sydney a number of mechanisms can be noted, including the establishment of special laws that give the strategic authority powers over developments in key sites, the establishment of Development Corporations controlled by the strategic authority, the setting up special ad hoc committees also controlled by the strategic authority and the reconfiguration of local authority boundaries to change their political composition and hence the chances of opposition. Some of these mechanisms, such as the Development Corporation, have of course been used in London in the past. It will be interesting to see how the need to ensure the implementation of a strategy to improve the competitiveness of London will be satisfied within the new GLA arrangements. What effect will the new emphasis on transparency and greater democracy have on this process?

Agenda-Setting in the GLA

The GLA will be required to combine the aims of economic competitiveness, environmental sustainability and social cohesion. The government seems to assume that the establishment of a single strategic authority will enable these aims to be combined and integrated. A key role of the Authority will be to employ joined-up thinking and co-ordinate objectives and policy across these different spheres. There is an inherent belief here in the ability to create some kind of institutional arrangements that will allow for agreement. This belief in the ability to generate consensus reflects the sentiments expressed by Blair in his 'Third Way'. In his Fabian Pamphlet he explains that his vision is to 'reconcile themes which in the past have been regarded as antagonistic' (1998, p.1). One of these antagonisms that can be resolved under the Third Way is that between 'the promotion of enterprise and the attack on poverty and discrimination'. A similar stance is taken in London Study (ALG, 1999) in which a diagram is constructed to show that the resolution of the three objectives can be achieved through an overlapping win-win zone. The ALG study recognises that there are tensions between the different agendas but states that these can be overcome through a negotiated consensus.

A contrasting view would suggest that the aims of economic competitiveness, environmental sustainability and social cohesion contain within them conflicts of interest that inevitably clash. Indeed this may not be just between the three agendas but also within each one. As Gordon points out in his contribution to this volume (see Chapter Two) there are different economic interests contained within the competitiveness agenda. Conflicts have been evident in many cities, for example the expansion of airports to promote a city's World City potential creates noise that impacts on resident's quality of life (it is noteworthy in this respect that the GLA will be required to produce both a strategy for economic development and one for ambient noise). The literature suggests that one impact of expanding 'World City' economic functions is to increase social polarisation (e.g. Sassen, 1991). The need for short-term economic benefits in a competitive environment can also lead to the sacrifice of some longer term environmental objectives. Can it be assumed that a compromise can be found to satisfy all such interests? If development land is in short supply then different interests such as residents and commercial developers will be in direct competition for that land. Establishing consensus and compromise will be a tough proposition and place considerable strain on the institutional arrangements for achieving it. Even where interests are not in direct conflict and a compromise can be achieved there is no 'natural position' for a balanced solution. Power and influence will be crucial in determining exactly where the 'balance' is struck. This will be determined by the interplay between the Mayor, interest groups, political representatives at Borough and GLA level, and Central Government. How will these forces be mediated through the new GLA structures and how will the resultant 'balance' compare to the practice of the last ten years?

Theoretically one could imagine that the approach to this agenda setting stage could take a number of forms. Four models are suggested below, although the reality of course is not likely to be this neat:

The 'regime' approach

This would involve the establishment of coalitions of interests. The arrangements could be fairly informal and based on networks of influence. The composition of the 'regime' of interests could take different forms and involve different degrees of power and influence for the various interests, who might operate in various forms of partnership with the GLA.

The institutional approach

This could be highly orchestrated with the establishment of structures for debate over aims and priorities. This would require a hands on attitude from the GLA. Mechanisms for conflict resolution would need to be established. Emphasis would be given to how these arrangements would link into the scrutiny role of the Assembly and the annual public hearings.

The strong leader approach

In this case the co-ordination would be achieved through the Mayor imposing his/her individual authority on all strategies. This would involve a Mayor taking a very clear approach to the development of priorities or emphasising a few very high profile policies which then inform all others.

The ad-hoc approach

This would result from little consideration being given to the issue of priorities and potential conflicts between aims. It would be characterised by an approach that simply responded to pressures exerted by different bodies, allowing the 'divisions' of the GLA to operate more or less independently, and placing a heavy reliance on the adoption of readily available research and policy ideas in an ad hoc manner.

In setting the agenda the GLA will need to establish priorities within each of the three aims of economic competitiveness, environmental sustainability and social cohesion. It will also have to resolve any conflicts between the three aims and try and co-ordinate the different policies and strategies that are produced. It will have to conduct this activity at three different levels:

- *Within the 'divisions'* The task of each 'division' of the GLA, such as Transport for London or the LDA, contains a range of different aims. It will be necessary to make choices over priorities.

- *Within the GLA* The formulation of priorities in the GLA's overarching strategic co-ordinating functions such as the SDS and the pursuit of sustainability. This would include how the various 'divisions' of the authority, such as LDA and Cultural Strategy team etc. are integrated into this broader process.

- *Between the GLA and outside bodies* To what degree will the agenda of the GLA be influenced by the views of outside bodies? These bodies could include central government, the Boroughs and different pressure groups. How will the regional dimension impinge on the agenda?

Some Questions for the GLA and LDA

Some of the implications of the above discussion lead to the formulation of three central questions relating to the future approach of the GLA and the LDA.

1. How will the agendas of the different strategies be coordinated?

The GLA has the responsibility to produce eight different statutory strategies: spatial development, transport, economic development, air quality, ambient noise, waste management, bio-diversity, and culture. One major issue will be how these eight strategies are coordinated to establish the joined-up thinking that the government requires. There will be considerable overlap in the content of some of these strategies - for example Economic Development and Culture both cover tourism - but will they necessarily be pursuing the same priorities? Of particular interest is the relationship between the Economic Development Strategy and the Spatial Development Strategy. Will one of these have a dominant role over the other? Two possibilities (amongst others) can be suggested (see Figure 5.1).

Figure 5.1
Potential Relationships Between the Economic Development Strategy & Spatial Development Strategy

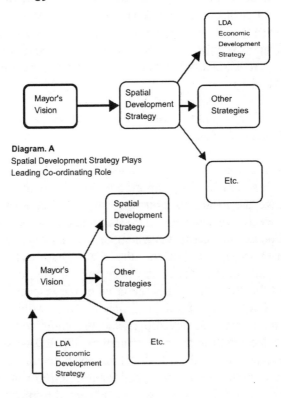

Diagram. A
Spatial Development Strategy Plays
Leading Co-ordinating Role

Diagram. B
London Development Agency has Strong Influence on Overall Priorities

- The Mayor would develop his/her vision and this would be presented in the SDS, which would then have a coordinating function for the whole of the GLA objectives and strategies. One government statement seems to suggest this when it says that 'it will set priorities and provide direction for the future development of London, and will be integrated with the Mayor's other strategies including those for transport, economic development and the environment' (DETR - London governance fact sheets) (see Figure 5.1a).

- Drawing on the experience of Sydney and Singapore, a second possibility would be that the city marketing vision exerts a strong influence over the spatial strategic plans. In this case the city marketing role of the LDA would lead to an influence over the Mayor's vision and the SDS would then simply translate this into land use and development terms (see Figure 5.1b).

2. How will the LDA ensure that its strategy on economic development is implemented?

The message from Sydney and Singapore is that if the strategic authority is serious about promoting economic competitiveness it has to have the means to overcome any local opposition. How will this evolve in the new GLA structure? Who will have the ultimate power to decide what happens on strategic sites? The issue of how much control the GLA has over strategic development control decisions was one of the controversial aspects of the Bill. This raises the issue of the respective roles of Borough, GLA and central government. How would conflicts, such as those between developers and the community in Kings Cross, be dealt with in the new structure? The LDA has a strong role in relation to land with development potential through its responsibilities to promote competitiveness, ensure regeneration and prepare sites. However it will be subjected to pressures from the rest of the GLA, the Boroughs responding to community pressures, and central government with its own agenda, e.g. promoting maximum house-building on brown field sites. It will be interesting to see how these different pressures are brought to bear and how they are resolved (see Figure 5.2).

Figure 5.2
Pressures on the LDA's Agenda of Priorities

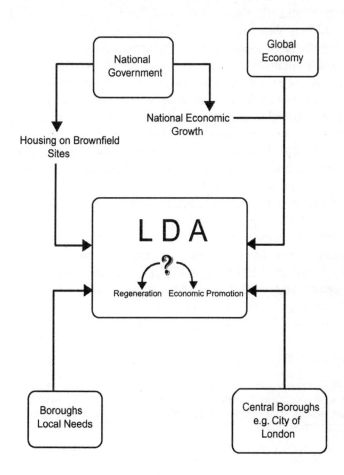

3. How will the agenda priorities be determined within the LDA itself?

Within the GLA there are likely to be different views emanating from a number of directions, such as those of small business and those of international finance companies. One of the most interesting to observe will be the resolution of the competition objective and the regeneration objective. The first will be oriented to global economic pressures while the other will need to be responsive to local interests. Perhaps the two strands will be pursued in separate compartments and the interrelationships never addressed (see Colenutt, chapter 8). The LDA is required to be a business-led organisation and this will be reflected in its board membership. What impact will this have on the balance between competition and regeneration? How will such a business-led organisation fit into the GLA as a whole with the rather different pressures coming from the Mayor, the Assembly's scrutiny role and the annual public hearings?

All these questions will need to be investigated once the GLA is up and running. The governance of London is definitely undergoing change. However it is probably not being too presumptuous to say that, whatever happens, it will continue to be a highly complex business. Whether it will be more transparent and democratic remains to be seen.

Notes

[1] Such an investigation is being undertaken in relation to planning and sustainability by Andy Thornley and Yvonne Rydin in an ESRC funded research project entitled, 'Institutional Change, Networks and Agendas: Planning under the GLA' (R000223095).

References

Association of London Government, (1999) *The London Study*, London, ALG.

Blair, T. (1996) *New Britain: My Vision of a Young Country*, London, Fourth Estate.

Blair, T. (1998) *The Third Way: New Politics for the New Century*, London, Fabian Society.

Chua, B.H. (1998) 'World cities, globalisation and the spread of consumerism: a view from Singapore, *Urban Studies*, vol.35, no.5/6, pp.981-1000.

Department of Planning (1995) *Cities for the 21st Century*, Sydney, Department of Planning.

Department of Environment Transport and the Regions (2000) *London Governance: Factsheets*, www.detr.gov.uk. 28/01/00.

Giddens, A. (1994) *Beyond Left and Right*, Cambridge, Polity Press.

Giddens, A. (1998) *The Third Way: The Renewal of Social Democracy,* Cambridge, Polity Press.

Held, D., McGrew, A., Goldblatt, D. and Perraton, J. (1999) *Global Transformation*, Cambridge, Polity Press.

Judd, D.R. (1999) 'Constructing the tourist bubble', in D.R. Judd and S. Fainstein, *The Tourist City*, New Haven, University of Yale Press, pp.35-53.

London Pride Partnership (1995) *The London Pride Prospectus*, London, LPP.

Newman, P. and Thornley, A. (1997) 'Fragmentation and centralisation in the governance of London: influencing the urban policy and planning agenda', *Urban Studies*, vol.34, no.7, pp.967-988.

Sassen, S. (1991) *The Global City*, New Jersey, Princeton University Press.

Searle, G. (1996) *Sydney as a Global City*, Sydney, Department of Planning.

Chapter 6

The Potential Role of the LDA in London's Economic Regeneration

ERIC SORENSON

Introduction

The forerunner to the London Development Agency (LDA), the London Development Partnership (LDP), functioned for a limited two year period up until the LDA began operation in July 2000. The LDP was set up by pan London bodies from trade unions, education, the voluntary sector and private business, with the aim of helping the Mayor hit the ground running in terms of thinking about London's economic development issues. The LDP was closely tied to the LDA in that it addressed the eight strategies for the regions (i.e. spatial development, transport, economic development, air quality, ambient noise, waste management, bio-diversity, and culture) that all of the other English Regional Development Agencies (RDAs) which started their operation a year earlier in April, 1999, had already produced.

The Greater London Authority (GLA) Act was used by government to tackle many issues, rather at the whim of those constructing the Act (DETR, 1998). As a result, under the Act there are widespread requirements of the LDA as represented by the many strategy requirements. This fits with the determination of the government to approach life holistically. The LDP approach was to develop a number of manifestos relating to London, primarily focusing on economic development issues. It was supported by other parallel activities including those in the areas of private finance, business development (working with the City Corporation/Greater London Enterprise) and social inclusion (in association with the London Voluntary Sector Council). Other manifestos developed by the LDP were in the areas of skills, innovation and knowledge transfer, manufacturing support, EU funding, as well as an overall economic development strategy for London (LDP, March, 1999). The end product of this activity was a series of reports for the Mayor which he was under no obligation to make any use of.

Based on the experience gained from the operation of the LDP, this chapter focuses on two key issues. First, the nature of the LDA as an institution, and second, the economic challenges presented by London with which the LDA must deal.

The Nature of the LDA

The LDA is one of a family of RDAs, but unlike the others it is not a quango, but a Mayoral agency with the Mayor appointing the board/executive of the LDA. There are loose structural guidances that ensure that the make up of the LDA will address the interests of various groups, such as the private and voluntary sectors. Under such a set up the Mayor and his appointees are of critical importance in establishing the direction of the LDA. Whilst the legislation of the RDAs was merely added into the GLA Act, in the case of London this combination has created a situation where the Mayor has considerable power over what this new institutional animal does.

The brief for the RDAs is about economic competitiveness, social inclusion and the care of the environment through sustainability. Phrases such as 'social inclusion' and 'sustainability' have only really become common terms in recent years. Sustainability is a particularly elusive concept which is sometimes used for environmental issues, but is also more widely used, such as in relation to the promotion of employment and the reduction of unemployment which is regarded as a key component of economic sustainability in an urban society. Consequently it is a broad concept that is in danger of becoming too all embracing and merely a rather meaningless phrase relating to a better quality of life.

Given this context it is worthwhile questioning what the LDA is actually intended for. Three possible scenarios for the LDA include:

1. A focus on business growth and diversity in London.
2. A focus on a traditional physical regeneration role of exploiting brown field opportunities and changing the economic geography of the urban area, utilising reward systems relating to the numbers of bricks built and leverage rates of private investment.
3. A focus on a more fine-grained community based approach, working with community enterprise and businesses. It could work with the New Deal for Communities initiative in trying to erode the appalling spatial deprivation that exists in London.

These three models of approach can all be performed in a way that meets the tests of competitiveness, social inclusion and sustainability. They are not incompatible. However the balance between them will be important in defining what the LDA is going to stand for. With regard to creating an institution appropriate to pursuing its own vision, the initial staffing of the LDA appears problematic. From the first of April 2000 the transfer of staff from existing institutions to the LDA began. These transfers included a group of staff working in the Single Regeneration Budget (SRB) area who were moved from programme management work in the Government Office for London (GOL); a large group of surveyors moved across from English Partnerships London City Region; and a number of planners from GOL. In total these groups accounted for a large proportion of the 90 staff that the LDA initially employed. As a consequence the early staffing structure comprised a large number of surveyors and SRB managers even before it was clear what the 'hapless animal' would do. A primary task for the LDA will therefore be to clarify what its role is and create an organisational culture appropriate to this end.

A second key point concerning the LDA's structure is that although there has been much talk about 'joined up' working, in practice, Whitehall being a series of baronies that are led by Secretaries of State, is a federal institution. This is manifest in the creation of the LDA, where other new institutions such as the Small Business Service (SBS) have been set up and will run separately and in parallel with the LDA under the auspices of separate government departments; in this case the Department of Trade and Industry. Similarly the Learning and Skills Councils (LSCs), which will be more important than the Training and Enterprise Councils (TECs) given their responsibility for the funding of Further Education, are also run separately under the auspices of the Department for Education and Employment. This is despite the fact that the LDA has a responsibility to produce London-wide economic business and skills strategies. In this situation there is a risk that strategy making will go on in one place (the LDA), but the operational power and the money will be elsewhere (e.g. in the SBS and the five local LSCs). The challenge of joining this all up is considerable.

A third key factor relating to the institutional changes taking place within London is finance. Changes are usually oiled with cash. For example, Margaret Thatcher's reforms of the National Health Service, regardless of whether they worked, were well financed. The London government structure is not being oiled with cash. The LDA has inherited the English Partnership funding stream and the SRB funding (circa £300 million per annum) but little else – yet it has a great many responsibilities. The situation is even more fluid with respect to transport where there remains an ongoing debate over how to find the funding needed to tackle core upgrading and development work, notably in respect of the underground.

Economic Challenges Facing the LDA

The sheer scale of London makes it a varied city where generalisations can easily be deceptive (see Figure 6.1). Many statistics about London are either misleading or wrong. Given the diversity of London, statistics can be selected from specific areas with specific criteria in order to construct almost any argument.

London's gross domestic product is 140% of the UK average, within the City and West End this figure is over 400%, and yet in the outer East and North East this figure drops to around 70%. Indeed, there are pockets of concentrations of considerable deprivation, with London containing 13 of the 20 most deprived boroughs in England (LDP, 2000).

Based on a diagram from London Pride Partnership 1995

Figure 6.1 Population Comparison of London Boroughs with Major UK Towns and Cities

In relation to the long term economic decline of traditional industries, London has suffered just as much as the Northern cities. Whereas Sheffield suffered from the decline of steel, Newcastle from the decline of shipbuilding and Manchester from the decline of textiles, the same deindustrialisation processes were operating within London. To some extent such processes were shielded by the size and diversity of the London economy which includes growth sectors such as finance, business services, tourism and hospitality. The fact is that London lost one million jobs between 1974-1994 (LDP, 2000), particularly in the historic industrial corridors of the Thames Gateway, Lee Valley (where jobs are still being lost in the Southern part), the Western Approaches around the A4 and M4, and also the Wandle Valley. In these area there are brownfield sites that can be redeveloped and will form an important priority for future economic development.

With regard to macro economic trends, a key feature is London's increasing population. This rate of increase would be higher if housing output was raised to the UK average. It is unclear why housing output is so low, although the high cost of housing is clearly preventing key workers such as nurses and teachers moving into London. If future housing growth is planned in line with the Richard Rogers (1999) 'Urban Renaissance' model of high population density around transport nodes, the population of London could be increased considerably beyond the present projected increase of around 600,000 between 1991-2011. In these circumstances, announcements of a massive house building programme in London and the South East, together with special provision for key worker housing at affordable prices, is a welcome step forward.

A second key macro economic trend is in the central areas, including the City and Canary Wharf and also to the West in Hammersmith and further extending to Heathrow (an important generator of around 200,000 jobs). Here, there is an agglomeration effect with business and job activities concentrated in these areas. The central area is of course changing. Recent developments such as the Globe Theatre and Tate Modern exemplify the huge growth of culturally driven visitor attractions, in areas such as the South Bank and Lambeth. This is pulling the central area of London across the Thames. There is a further move South across the river via the major development now taking place in the Elephant and Castle and the possible continuation of the sweep round to Nine Elms and Battersea.

Business services comprise such an agglomeration of different business activities that we need to be careful in our analysis of this sector. Whilst we have already noted the shift from manufacturing to business service activities across London, we need to disaggregate our analyses of business service activities in order to understand how this is impacting upon different parts of London. For example, if we examine the financial services component, the Corporation of London (1999) research into the competitiveness of this sector distinguished between 'proximal' retail financial services (e.g. retail banks), 'non proximal' support services (e.g. information technology), and 'City' trades (e.g. international finance). Although, overall financial services are likely to grow at around 2% per annum for the next three years in London (London Economic Review, 1999), this is likely to be uneven, with further shake-out of employment due to rationalisation and technological changes, notably in retail banking. The IT software sector does appear set for further growth, both in relation to financial services and more generally within the business services sector (Westminster Council, 1998). The City of London remains a major global financial centre, and a merger with another major financial centre such as Frankfurt should enable it to retain its premier position in Europe and competitiveness against New York and Tokyo.

There is massive job displacement in the London labour market with over 650,000 commuters (LDP, 2000), representing one fifth of London's work force. This matter is exacerbated by the high proportion (26%) of Londoners that have no or very low qualifications with, on the whole, commuters tending to be more highly qualified (35% of Londoners are degree educated compared with 44% of commuters).

London is an open city. It is international and multi-cultural, containing almost half (48%) of the UK's ethnic minority population (Focus on London, 1999). This figure is forecast to increase, with London's ethnic population expected to rise from 24% to 28% during the next decade.

A map of London 30 years ago would indicate broadly similar problem areas as we see today, with concentrations of deprivation in the North and East along the Lee Valley and Thames Gateway areas, to the West in Brent, Ealing and Hammersmith and Fulham, and to the South along the Wandle

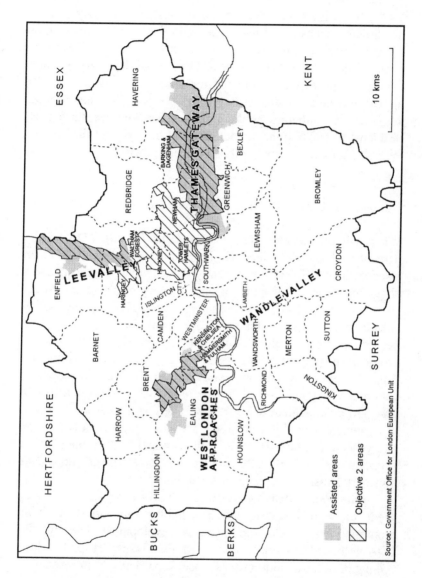

**Figure 6.2 London Objective 2 and Assisted Areas 2000-2006
and Regeneration Gateways**

Valley (see Figure 6.2). We may conclude that urban regeneration has failed, because little has changed in the intensity or location of deprivation. This is not quite true, because there are countervailing forces taking place. The map of deprivation is also a map of the residualisation of the social housing sector. We appear to have a perverse policy where the poor are ghettoised as a matter of deliberate public policy. Therefore we face great problems in tackling the serious issue of how we get the poorest people to jobs which are not located near to them.

Conclusion: Future Priorities for the LDA

What will be the emerging spatial focus for the LDA? Sixty percent of brownfield land in the South East of England is in London, of which 28% is currently developable. Given concerns about brownfield development and housing needs in the South East, the Thames Gateway is set to rise rapidly up the policy agenda, particularly as this area, along with the Lee Valley, will be in receipt of European Union funding. West London also has problems, displaying all the worst characteristics of an edge city. This area has an incoherence and form of anarchic development which is worrying, particularly in relation to sorting out public transport development to Heathrow. There is a clear need to take key strategic spatial development decisions more rapidly. It took five years to decide what to do with Terminal 5. How can London maintain itself as a globally competitive city when such important transport decisions are delayed for so long?

In the poorer areas where funding will be targeted, the focus needs to be on creating efficient public transport as well as promoting brownfield and business development. Clearly, the LDA will need to work together with the 'Transport for London' agency in order to address these issues, particularly in respect of facilitating pathways for getting London's poorest residents to the work place.

This chapter has presented a broad overview of some of the key issues facing the LDA. In the early stages of its development it will be critically important to clarify what the organisation will do, and this in turn will need to feed into the skills mix required of its personnel. What is clear, is that a set of people with a background in public sector management do not appear best suited to tackle the kind of economic development issues currently faced by London.

References

Corporation of London (1999) *The Competitiveness of London's Financial and Business Service Sector*, London, CoL.

Department of Environment Transport and Regions (DETR) (1998) *London Government The White Paper A Mayor and Assembly for London*, London, DETR.

Focus on London (1999) *Focus on London 99*, London, Crown Copyright.

London Development Partnership (2000) *Building London's Economy*, London, LDP.

Rogers, R. (1999) *Towards an Urban Renaissance*, London, DETR.

The London Economic Review (1999) *Report First Quarter*, London, LCCI.

Westminster City Council (1998) *Sector Review*, London, BSL.

Chapter 7

Strategy and Partnership: Governing London in the Millennium

NICK BAILEY

Introduction

The trend towards urban governance over the last 20 years is best illustrated by the rhetoric which stresses that partnership is now the only way to deliver effective, joined-up policy 'which works'. This is particularly true in the field of urban regeneration where in all urban and many rural areas there is a profusion of partnerships of all kinds operating at all levels. Early examples emerged in the 1980s both as a result of proactive initiatives by business interests (CBI, 1988) and through innovative local authority initiatives, such as in Birmingham and Greenwich (Bailey et al., 1995). Others emerged in response to European funding, the actual or imagined threat of Urban Development Corporations, and the Conservative government's City Pride initiative. A more typical model emerged in the 1990s with the arrival of City Challenge and the Single Regeneration Budget (SRB). To these should be added a slightly different approach in response to the New Deal for Communities.

It is possible therefore to identify four broad phases of partnership formation:

1. Early experiments where different stakeholders developed coalitions of interests and joint strategies towards specific areas;
2. Partnerships formed in response to government policy and in order to access resources allocated on a competitive basis or in order to promote economic development and inward investment;

3. Partnerships led by the public or private sectors to develop comprehensive strategies for defined areas including economic development, social inclusion and regeneration;
4. The establishment of networks of partnerships, operating at different levels and with clearly defined geographical and policy boundaries, in order to promote a strategic approach at the city, regional or sub-regional and local levels.

It will be argued in this paper that the first two phases above have evolved in an ad hoc and piecemeal fashion operating as a patchy mosaic across large parts of the country. In the case of the third category there are many good examples of strategic approaches at the urban or sub-regional scales. Coventry and Warwickshire Partnership Limited, The Thames Gateway Partnership and the East London Partnership are just three examples.

We are now entering the fourth phase with the arrival of the Regional Development Agencies (RDAs) where it is likely that considerable rationalisation of partnership arrangements will be needed. The situation in London is inevitably more complicated given its size, economic complexity and the evolution of institutional arrangements which can be traced back to the abolition of the Greater London Council (Bailey, 1997). The time has come when partnerships must be 'outward-looking', able to operate both top-down and bottom-up as part of an extended network, and contribute towards the definition and achievement of a broader strategy.

The Political and Economic Imperative for Partnership

There is an extensive literature on the impact of globalisation and the possibility that we are entering a period of Post-Fordist production and consumption (Burrows and Loader, 1994). These trends are having a profound effect on the UK economy and London is now identified as one of three or four leading World Cities (Llewelyn-Davies et al., 1996). One of the leading commentators in the field is Bob Jessop who contrasts the

Keynesian Welfare State with what he calls the Schumpeterian Workfare State:

> "Its distinctive objectives in economic and social reproduction are: to promote product, process, organisational and market innovation in open economies in order to strengthen as far as possible the structural competitiveness of the national economy by intervening on the supply-side; and to subordinate social policy to the needs of labour market flexibility and/or to the constraints of international competition" (Jessop, 1994, p.24).

He goes on to suggest that with the globalisation of economic forces, the nation-state is being 'hollowed out':

> "Thus we find that the powers of nation-states are being limited through a complex displacement of powers upward, downward and outward. Some state capacities are transferred to an increasing number of pan-regional...or international bodies with a widening range of powers; others are devolved to restructured local or regional levels of governance within the nation-state; and yet others are being usurped by emerging horizontal networks of power – local and regional – which by-pass central states and connect localities or regions in several nations" (Jessop, 1994, pp.24-25).

This clearly has immediate relevance for trends in the 1990s towards regionalisation, the increasing importance of Europe as an economic and political institution and the transfer of power and resources to agents of urban governance such as partnerships. Equally important for the development of partnerships has been the devolution of power to the Scottish Parliament and the Welsh and Northern Ireland Assemblies. New institutions have also emerged to promote economic and social development in the regions, and in London the GLA and an elected Mayor may provide a model which will spread to other UK cities.

Harvey has also written extensively on the 'transformation in urban governance in late capitalism' (Harvey 1989). In reviewing trends in both Europe and the USA, he notes a transition from 'managerialism to entrepreneurialism in urban governance' and that public-private partnership is a common element in very different political and legal contexts:

> "First, the new entrepreneurialism has, as its centrepiece, the notion of 'public-private partnership' in which a traditional local boosterism is integrated with the use of local governmental powers to try and attract external sources of funding, new direct investments, or new employment sources......Secondly, the activity of that public-private partnership is entrepreneurial precisely because it is speculative in execution and design and therefore dogged by all the difficulties and dangers that attach to speculative as opposed to rationally planned and co-ordinated development". (Harvey, 1989, p.7).

The precise balance of economic, social and political forces underlying the deep-seated trends in governance must remain conjectural but there is extensive evidence that the trend towards establishing coalitions and partnerships in most advanced economies is now well underway. There is also evidence that Britain is at the forefront of developments in multi-sectoral partnerships at the regional and city levels (Carley and Kirk, 1999).

Carley and Kirk conclude that a successful city-wide regeneration strategy is dependent on a high quality strategic partnership. 'The strategy derives from mutual learning among equal partners, in analysing problems and devising solutions' (Carley and Kirk, 1999, p. 65). The strategy should have two essential components:

- an *economic and sustainable development strategy* at the level of either the city or travel-to-work sub-region.
- an *operational regeneration strategy* that secures funding and manages area-based regeneration and related projects, and provides the necessary public accountability. (Carley and Kirk, 1999, p.74).

The North Kent/Thames Gateway Experience

In carrying out research on partnership formation in that part of the Thames Gateway lying in Kent, Whitehead (1999) found a profusion of partnerships at different levels but with apparently overlapping remits and responsibilities which: 'appear to lack a logical and coherent structure in terms of areas of coverage and partnership function'. There are at least five partnerships operating at county or regional levels; eleven at the sub-regional level; nine covering local authority districts or towns; and three representing individual communities (Whitehead, 1999, p.51).

In a questionnaire sent to leading members of each partnership, 70% said that a strategy existed for the region but respondents identified five different documents. 50% of respondents listed the Thames Gateway Planning Framework (RPG9a). Whitehead notes that this 'is relatively vague and loosely worded and focuses on a wider area than the Kent area of the Gateway' (Whitehead 1999, p.52). One interviewee is reported as saying:

"I personally get immensely frustrated by the complexities of some of these partnerships, not simply that they are complex in themselves but in terms of how their agendas overlap. There isn't sufficient liaison between them, in order that they are not getting in each others way". (Whitehead, 1999, p.53).

Evidence of overlapping responsibilities is cited in that both North Kent Success and North Kent Joint Consultative Committee aim to provide a forum for the development of a strategy in order to progress the regeneration of that part of the Thames Gateway in North Kent. In addition, both the Kent Thames-side Association and the Kent Thames-side Joint Executive Committee seek to develop a co-ordinated development strategy for the Kent Thames-side area.

Whitehead concludes that there is evidence of both duplication of tasks and a lack of co-ordination amongst partnerships, although this is off set to some degree by informal networking between partnership members and joint membership of different bodies held by key officers and members. 'It is in fact the lack of a coherent organisational structure and the lack of a hierarchy of partnership responsibilities that have created an inefficient approach' (Whitehead, 1999, p. 65). It is suggested that the South East Economic Development Agency (SEEDA), which was launched in April 1999, has a major role to play in developing a regional strategy, to which all can subscribe, and in formalising roles and relationships between the existing partnerships.

Partnerships in London

Partnerships have developed in London in an ad hoc fashion similar to that in the Thames Gateway, largely since the demise of the Greater London Council in the mid-1980s. However, in London there have been relatively free-standing initiatives by both the public and private sectors. At the city wide level, the London Development Partnership (LDP) was the shadow body set up to prepare the way for the establishment of the London Development Agency (LDA) in 2000. Below this level the private sector has taken the lead in forming the West London Leadership and the East London Partnership. There are less well established business leadership teams in North and South London.

The public sector, on the other hand, has focused on areas of declining manufacturing industry and multiple deprivation. These include the London Lee Valley Partnership, overlapping with the Thames Gateway London Partnership, and more recently the Wandle Valley Partnership. The Central London Partnership brings together leading London-based companies, members of eight boroughs, and representatives of the Metropolitan Police and London Transport. The dynamic behind the public sector partnerships tend to be the availability of European Objective 2 funding and from the Single Regeneration Budget. In practice, both public and private sector-led partnerships draw their membership from both sectors. Below this level there are a large number of partnerships operating at the borough or district levels (for example town centres) and 243 partnerships responsible for six rounds of SRB (see Table 7.1). In addition, London now has five local Learning and Skills Councils (LSCs), London Business Link with five sub-regional offices, and 16 health authorities. Most of these are heavily involved in partnership activities in the capital.

Table 7.1 Single Regeneration Budget Partnerships in London, 1995-2001

Round	Year	Number of schemes approved	Funding
1	1995-96	48	£316m
2	1996-97	41	£230m
3	1997-98	48	£280m
4	1998-99	22	£73m
5	1999-00	38	£320m
6	2000-01	46	£300m
Total	1995-01	243	£1519m

Source: Government Office for London

Since 1994 the Government Office for London has played a key role in co-ordinating investment in the capital's infrastructure and the promotion of economic development and training. However, its decision-making is relatively opaque and accountability is limited. The key issues facing partnerships are:

- The lack of an overall economic and regeneration strategy for the capital.
- The fragmentation of responsibilities and differential time scales in relation to key policy areas such as planning, regeneration, infrastructure and transport.
- The difficulties of addressing issues which cross borough boundaries or require a joined-up approach, for example, health, housing and employment.

- The lack of involvement of the voluntary and community sectors in strategic partnerships.
- The difficulty of achieving continuity and accountability in an unstable policy environment.
- Uneven coverage of partnerships at different levels and in different locations.
- The need to reflect and act on local aspirations, meet local needs and to demonstrate effectiveness, efficiency and equity in delivery.

The Task Ahead for the London Development Agency

The arrival of the LDA, GLA and elected Mayor will add substantially to the capacity of partnerships to develop the capital's economy and promote regeneration, but will also add a new tier of agencies on top of those currently in existence. At present, it appears that the LDA will accept the current institutional framework and work through sub-regional and local partnerships rather than imposing a more rigid tiered system. Building on the LDP's groundwork (2000) the development of an economic strategy for London will be the focus of the LDA's early activity and this will need to be closely co-ordinated with the development of the Spatial Development Strategy (Hall, Edwards et al, 1999; Thornley, chapter five)

In a study commissioned by DETR (1998a) consultants suggested that the new RDAs would need to appraise the division of responsibilities and management capacity of existing partnerships as part of the process of developing a regional strategy. They also argued that solutions are likely to differ between regions. As a result of this analysis a number of questions that the regional strategies will need to address were identified (DETR, 1998b):

- What will the RDA expect of the sub-regional structure: contribution towards strategy formulation, delivery capacity or both?

- How does the RDA expect to approach issues of (unequal) sub-regional development?
- How will the RDA approach the definition of boundaries for sub-regions, especially where there are gaps in effective sub-regional coverage?
- Will the RDA introduce quality standards for partnerships, and how will they be enforced, particularly where partnerships are not in direct receipt of financial resources?
- What is the role for specialist regional networks in relation to the sub-regional networks?
- Will the RDA seek to eliminate the continuing duplications in delivery capacity at local or sub-regional level?
- How will the RDAs respond to the need to give priority to developing relatively undeveloped sub-regional partnerships, without neglecting those already well established?
- What role will the RDAs take in developing, across the region, the skills base needed for effective partnership-based approaches to economic development?

These are all particularly important questions for London. While being a major motor of the UK economy the capital contains large amounts of unemployment, social exclusion and large numbers lacking in basic educational qualifications and skills. At the same time it is made up of a patchwork quilt of partnerships with different remits, covering different geographical areas and with varying amounts of strategic vision and capacities to deliver.

Jessop's theory of the hollowing out of the state has considerable resonance for London at the beginning of the new millennium. At the strategic level, the capital now has an entirely new set of institutions with the capacity to operate across borough boundaries which will, no doubt, wish to work closely with adjoining organisations, such as the South East Economic Development Agency and the RDA in the East of England. These new institutions include: the elected Mayor, the GLA, the LDA, the Metropolitan Police Authority, Transport for London, the London Fire and Emergency Planning Authority and five local Learning and Skills Councils. The Mayor in particular has a wide remit and is charged with approving strategies for spatial development; transport; economic development; waste management; air quality; ambient noise; biodiversity and culture (GOL 2000).

One of the major legacies of the absence of strategic direction in London has been an accentuated pattern of uneven development in both the structure of the economy and in the institutional framework with the capacity to deliver a set of strategic solutions. The most likely scenario is that the Mayor, GLA and LDA will initially work through the existing institutional framework and then develop partnership capacities in the five sub-regions selected for the Learning and Skills Councils. Some rationalisation can therefore be anticipated.

Conclusions

For the past 15 years, London has suffered from the lack of a strategic vision and a fragmented and unaccountable system of government. Decisions regarding regeneration, the economy, education and skills, transport, infrastructure and health have been the responsibility of a host of bodies operating at different levels and with little integration between them. As we enter a new phase of partnership working within London there are a number of general questions which need to be addressed by new and existing agencies and partnerships at all levels:

- Will the various bodies be able to develop a strategic vision for the capital to which all can subscribe?
- How can the process of strategy building be made inclusive, transparent and responsive to sub-regional and local perspectives and needs?
- Given the extent of London's travel to work area and its dominant role in the South East, how can the strategy be made outward looking and integrated with adjoining regions? (section 342 of the Greater London Authority Act requires the Mayor to have regard to any regional planning guidance relating to adjoining areas)

- How can the boroughs be encouraged to buy-in to the process?
- How can the process be made more accountable to stakeholders, London residents and employees?
- Are two levels of regeneration policy emerging, as Colenutt (1999, and chapter eight) suggests, with strategic bodies largely concerned with economic competitiveness, and a lower tier of needs-based local partnerships? If so, what more can be done to integrate the two levels?
- Perhaps the biggest challenge: how can differences of 'uneven development' (in terms of economic activity, service provision and institutional capacity) be diminished without constraining the most dynamic sectors of the economy and the most effective service-deliverers? How can the weakest partnerships be encouraged to acquire the attributes of the best?

Acknowledgement

I am very grateful to Maxine Jones of the London Development Agency for supplying additional information.

References

Bailey, N, Barker, A and MacDonald, K. (1995) *Partnership Agencies in British Urban Policy*, London, UCL Press.

Bailey, N. (1997) 'Competitiveness, partnership– and democracy? Putting the 'local' back into London government', *Local Economy*, vol.12, no.3, pp.205-218.

Burrows, R. and Loader, B. (eds) (1994) *Towards a Post-Fordist Welfare State?*, London, Routledge.

Carley, M and Kirk, K. (1999) *City-Wide Urban Regeneration: Lessons from Good Practice*, Central Research Unit, Edinburgh, Scottish Executive.

Carter, A. (2000) 'Strategy and partnership in urban regeneration', in Roberts, P and Sykes, H. (eds) *Urban Regeneration: A Handbook*, London, Sage, pp.37-58.

Confederation of British Industry (1988) *Initiatives Beyond Charity: Report of the CBI Task Force on Business and Urban Regeneration*, London, CBI.

Colenutt, B. (1999) 'New deal or no deal for people-based regeneration?' in Imrie, R and Thomas, H. (eds) *British Urban Policy* (second edition), London, Sage.

Department of Environment, Transport and Regions (DETR) (1998a) *Building Partnerships in the English Regions: A Study Report of Regional and Sub-Regional Partnerships in England*, London, DETR.

Department of Environment, Transport and Regions (DETR) (1998b) *Building Partnerships in the English Regions: A Good Practice Guide*, London, DETR.

Jessop, B. (1994) 'The transition to post-Fordism and the Schumpeterian workfare state', in Burrows, R and Loader, B (eds) *Towards a Post-Fordist Welfare State?*, London, Routledge.

Government Office for London (2000) *Strategic Planning in London. Draft Circular*, London, GOL.

Hall, P, Edwards, M et al. (1999) *London's Spatial Economy: The Dynamics of Change*, London, RTPI London Branch with the LDP.

Harvey, D. (1989) 'From managerialism to entrepreneurialism: the transformation in urban governance in late capitalism'. *Geografiska Annaler*, vol.71B, no.1, pp.3-17.

Llewelyn-Davies, UCL The Bartlett and Comedia (1996) *Four World Cities: A Comparative Study of London, Paris, New York and Tokyo*, London, Llewelyn-Davies.

London Development Partnership (2000) *Building London's Economy*, London, LDP.

Whitehead, K. (1999) 'Too many partnerships?' *Unpublished MA Dissertation in Town Planning*, London, University of Westminster.

Chapter 8

Will London Boroughs be Winners or Losers in the New Regional Structures for London?

BOB COLENUTT

Introduction

This paper explores the role of the local Boroughs in the new economic development structures for London. The Boroughs have expectations that, in the present political climate, they will benefit from the setting up of the London Development Agency (LDA), the Mayor's office and the Greater London Authority (GLA). But this outcome is by no means certain. There are several reasons for believing that the new government structures for London may not give them the support they need and expect.

Context

The London economy is booming – but not for all parts of the capital, and not all its residents. Poverty and lack of investment can be found in many Boroughs. Places like Tottenham, for example, have not experienced the recent property boom; investment in the housing and industrial stock is limited, major sites remain derelict and often these communities are transition zones for the poor and disadvantaged. Regeneration has made limited impact. The sheer pace of transition produces its own energy and enterprise, but deprivation is persistent. The Boroughs are struggling to meet demands for basic, and life and death services.

Alongside rapid economic change is the rapid change in local government itself. Modernisation is the prevalent ethos with 'best value', 'performance management', and restructuring being widespread whatever political party is in control. New duties for the economic and social well-being of residents are being introduced. However, the imperative in all sectors where local authorities still have responsibility (e.g. schools, environmental services, housing, and social services) is to improve efficiency in a climate of increased demand and rising expectations. All this must be done without increased resources. In fact, resources whether in people, capital or land, are being reduced.

Against this background lies uncertainty about the relationship between central and local government. Does central government trust local authorities? Many would say it does not (hence no additional money). At the very least, the jury is out. In this context will regional government be trusted any more? Judging by the way in which regional government in Wales and the English regions is evolving, there is significant control of regional structures and budgets by the political or administrative centre. London will be no different. The funding, powers and structures of London Government suggest tight control from Whitehall and from the political centre. In London, the Government Office for London (GOL) will still exercise significant control over the LDA, the planning system, and over grant regimes for European Union funding.

It is a depressing fact that the staffing of the LDA appears to be mainly transfers from existing government offices (see Sorenson, chapter six) thus creating little opportunity for fresh blood, new ideas or radical thinking. Much will depend on whether the Mayor's office and the GLA are able to stimulate a fresh debate about the economy of London and the role of the Boroughs.

Haringey Council Experience

Haringey is a classic case of a Borough with a two speed economy. It has a booming residential west end centred on Crouch End and Muswell Hill, and a much poorer area with low investment in the east, centred on Wood Green and Tottenham. Issues of poverty, homelessness, unemployment, low levels of educational achievement; and a large number of refugees and people from ethnic minorities and refugee communities must be addressed by government at every level. Haringey Council has applied successfully for regeneration grants of all kinds. Yet there are critical problems of how to ensure that local people, particularly those on low incomes, are seen to benefit. Moreover, there is no clear strategy for making regeneration sustainable in economic, environmental or area management terms.

The Council is heading rapidly down the path of modernisation set by the Government. It has a new cabinet structure (with the abolition of many committees and panels and replacement with lead members and a Policy and Strategy Committee). It has published a community plan, it has a full programme of 'best value' assessment. It is a 'New Commitment to Regeneration Authority' and has established a Borough-wide regeneration partnership with key stakeholders. It has published a regeneration strategy and set up a Haringey Regeneration Agency, which is managing a number of SRB programmes. There is a proliferation of strategic and local regeneration partnerships and it has set up town centre management and neighbourhood management initiatives.

The aims and programmes of the regeneration strategy mirror the Government's priorities (and those of the LDA):

- Competitiveness and sustainability
- Social exclusion
- Neighbourhood Renewal
- Partnership development.

The Council has been very successful with specific funding bids for SRB, European Regional Development Funds (ERDF), Sure Start, Employment Zones, and Home Office funds for CCTV. Its regeneration bids are focused on the 15 most deprived wards, all in the east of the Borough. The Borough has 5 out of the 60 Community Priority Areas identified by Government Office for London in London. Haringey is trying to join up the bids and funding streams in these areas, and at the same time, develop a neighbourhood renewal strategy. But this agenda does not bring in extra resources for front line services, nor does it solve long standing service delivery problems. In fact, budget cut-backs continue and there is widespread public dissatisfaction with some Council services.

London Borough's Expectations of Regional Government

No one believes that regional government is a panacea. Many of the economic and social problems, such as those in the east of the Borough of Haringey, are structural and deep-seated. London Government alone can have limited influence -- but it can help. The first expectation of the London Boroughs is that there will be improved access to funding opportunities (ERDF, SRB, Education, Health) to support local and Borough wide regeneration strategies. Alongside better access, there is a demand for more transparency about why some areas/projects get grants and others do not. This raises the question of which problems will be prioritised and what criteria for grant allocation will be used by the LDA and the Mayor (and GOL)? Will there be a fresh approach?

Second, the Boroughs expect a more coherent strategic approach on regeneration, planning, traffic and transport, the Thames and other waterways, on investment in major sites, and on business promotion. They expect their priorities to be supported by the LDA and other regional bodies. They also hope for support on the difficult issues of making regeneration sustainable and of funding Agenda 21 initiatives (for which there is little specific grant funding). Finally, the Boroughs want financial and political support for their sharp end local service delivery and area management problems.

What May Happen...

Papers from the Social Exclusion Unit are almost model statements of intent about regeneration policy with the Government looking to integrate economy and social exclusion and management within a participatory framework of accountability. Those RDA draft strategies that did not say this have been revised. But what will happen in practice? The first concern of the Boroughs is that strategic issues which are not in the remit of the LDA/Mayor, but of great importance to the Boroughs and their front line responsibilities, will be left out or not integrated (e.g. refugees, health, homelessness, education, ethnic minority business development).

Second, problems seen as 'local' (such as service delivery and area management problems) within the remit of the Boroughs may not be regarded as important by the regional level. There are already strong networks of government officials, public and private sector agencies at the strategic level working through London First and other bodies. They have a regional agenda which they have been pursuing for some years. Regional government may strengthen these networks and policy assumptions, leaving the local level to 'fend for themselves'.

Third, there is a strong likelihood that too much time may be spent by the region on strategy documents and statements and not enough on meaningful action. The first two years of regional government may be taken up with arguing about the details of strategy statements and establishing more and more regional partnerships. It is almost certain that the wheel will be reinvented several times over, while Borough-wide and neighbourhood action plans are neglected.

The worst case scenario is that pressure of market forces combined with the existing top-down London wide policy culture for regeneration will not deal with marginalisation of certain groups, nor will the LDA be willing to commit to significant resources or new thinking to neighbourhood-led regeneration. Intervention will be market driven focused on central London and key sites, without sufficient focus on sustainable development, equal opportunities, and people based regeneration. A pessimistic view is that there will be little change from the new structure itself, and that a radical change of focus will not be achieved only by pressure from residents, community groups and businesses from below

What Should Happen...

The Boroughs (and local people) must be able to ensure, through participation in strategic policy and decision making, that strategic planning and intervention does indeed meet their needs. In effect, local needs, local services and neighbourhood renewal must be integrated into strategic policy or there is a danger they will be sidelined; an outcome that would be to the eventual detriment of strategic objectives.

The main areas of local responsibility for Boroughs, such as homelessness, education, environmental services, community enterprise, support for ethnic minority businesses, Agenda 21, and sustainability are highly complex, usually contested, and require labour intensive solutions. This is the sharp end of regeneration. It is vital that the regional level gets involved in these problems, and acts as enabler, supporter and if necessary arbitrator.

The strategic level could lead the way in a radical change of direction by making direct revenue investment (with SRB funds, for example) in mainstream services in those target neighbourhoods. It could top up education resources in target areas, it could fund more waste collection, planning enforcement officers, housing and parks staff. Beyond this, it should champion and fund Community Development Trusts or neighbourhood investment banks; and could fund innovative Agenda 21 projects. Without this vision and commitment, a two-speed London economy, with its social divisions will continue - with London Boroughs left to pick up the pieces.

Chapter 9

Tackling Problems and Governing London: Urban Leaders' Views On What Needs To Be Done

SUSANNE MACGREGOR

Poverty and Excluded Communities in the London Mega-City

In this paper, London is viewed primarily as a megacity - the oldest megacity although now eclipsed by Mexico City, Sao Paulo, Tokyo and other growing conurbations. Manuel Castells has set the framework for analysis of such cities. He has argued (Castells, 1996) that today we live in a network society and network economy, one shaped by technological revolution, the informational revolution and the collapse of Soviet statism. Access to information and the nature of that information are key issues for the megacity and its inhabitants. The world and its citizens, he says, are divided between those included in this process and those who are excluded from it. Megacities are the new spatial form of the global economy and the emerging informational society. Their key features are size, speed of communication and diversity. 'It is this distinctive feature of being globally connected and locally disconnected, physically and socially, that makes megacities a new urban form' (Castells, 1996, p.404).

A striking feature of megacities, related to the above analysis, is the juxtaposition of extremes of wealth and poverty. The high-rise, glass-fronted office blocks, the hotels and cultural districts soar above poor estates, ghettoes and shanty towns. Within each megacity, there is both a third world city and a first world city. The internationally oriented business and corporate sector exists alongside a much poorer third world city of poverty, poor housing and a flourishing semi-legal and illegal informal economic sector.

These third world areas of large cities generally have higher rates of disease and mortality and many more problems of pollution than their first world counterparts. Megacities have particular problems because of their size and density, to do with transport, pollution, waste disposal and litter. In the megacities of the world, intense social problems linked to social disintegration are in evidence: homelessness, particularly of street children, drug abuse; violence; and crime. London is relatively stable and prosperous compared to other large cities but some of the social problems of polarisation and disorder are visible.

In Europe, currently, there is a renewed concern about poverty. Lawson (1993) has characterised the new poverty in the following way:

- Crystallisation of racial and ethnic divisions
- Downward turn in people's life chances
- Increased social and political isolation of the poor
- Increased risk of family breakdown
- More hostile and fearful relationships in local communities
- New forms of xenophobia and racism.

These problems intensified in the 1980s and 1990s as a result of changing economic, political, ideological and social conditions. There has been a growing trend for many inner city communities and outer city public housing estates in London (but also in other British cities and in cities across Europe) to be progressively cut off from mainstream labour market institutions and informal job networks. The new Labour government in Britain has selected tackling these problems as one of its main priorities.

The concept of social exclusion is very popular in debate at present, having replaced terms like poverty and the poor. The notions of inclusion and exclusion are integrally linked to the concept of community but all are problematic. When we talk of communities, are we talking about imagined communities, political constructions, or are we talking about defined spatial areas? How is membership defined and who decides who is to belong and who is to be excluded?

In continental Europe, the term social exclusion refers to social rights. It is assumed that citizens have social rights to employment, housing, health care and income protection. The question then is how is it that some people, especially the homeless and some of those living in certain areas, seem to have been confronted by barriers which exclude people from these rights? Policy responses thus focus on the idea of breaking down physical barriers, in the form of lack of transport facilities, or social barriers like stigma and poor services, especially schools, which operate to entrench social divisions. Policy debate concentrates on the issue of gaps: the gap between the one-parent and the two income family; the gap between the inner city and the suburbs; the gap between the school failures and the university graduates; the gap between white people and those from minority ethnic groups.

Reversing the processes of exclusion involves action at a number of different levels. Firstly, the environment can be improved through new buildings, refurbishment, better architecture and design, and awareness of issues of pollution and waste disposal, greening, air quality and so on. Secondly, the economic issues of unemployment and loss of jobs must be taken up through educational and training initiatives and local job creation schemes. Thirdly, poverty and powerlessness have to be attacked. Community empowerment may be the solution. The social psychological issues of disillusion and hopelessness have to be tackled through imaginative schemes of community involvement and self-help. Recognition of the limited nature of initiatives is important – not to expect too much from them but to recognise that small actions can make a difference to some people, and that it is possible to develop successful models of action which may then be extended more widely.

Current UK Government Policy on Communities and Cities

Cities generate intense wealth and poverty cheek by jowl (Power, 1999). As Anne Power, advisor to the government's Social Exclusion Unit and Professor of Social Policy at LSE, states:

'Governments play a critical role in attempting to order, equalise, integrate and smooth the rough ride of urban progress'. Yet, after 25 years of attempts at regeneration, poor neighbourhoods are still poor, council estates are unpopular, crime, dirt and noise continue – what has gone wrong?

A range of policies have focused on deprived neighbourhoods, especially council estates: Housing Action Areas; Estate Action; Safer Cities City Challenge. Some interventions create new problems as they target others. Power concludes that continuous intervention and effort is needed in these areas; not short term interventions as many programmes in recent years have been. The government's New Deal for Communities is one response to these challenges. The main elements of the policy are: target small areas with special resources; attract partners from private, community and voluntary sectors into the regeneration programme; encourage more flexible and action-oriented culture in local authorities; improve co-ordination between agencies and authorities and departments.

Most inner London boroughs are amongst the most deprived areas in the UK in spite of their location in the richest region. Recently a national newspaper reported the results of a survey of Londoners (Coote, 1999). This poll showed that residents of the capital think their city is an unhealthy place to live in, compares poorly to other UK cities and is likely to be even less healthy in five years time. There is evidence to support this view. Infant mortality rates in inner London are among the worst in Europe (7.3 deaths up to the age of one per 1,000 live births), deaths from pneumonia are high in inner London, as are deaths from suicide or injury, lung disease and stroke.

So London has many serious social problems to address. But at the same time these dismal portraits of life in the city should not overwhelm us. The megacity offers a larger range of choices than found in the countryside or in previous centuries and a vibrant, exciting, rich mix of pleasures. Food, music, languages, cultures, styles, clothes in a constantly shifting and colourful kaleidoscope.

The issue is 'how to rescue the poorest areas that sink to the bottom of the urban hierarchy affecting at least a quarter of city neighbourhoods' (Power, 1999) and give them access to the resources of the city. Other issues identified by government are: how to change the skills of the population to meet the new job demands of the service and information economy; how to reduce crime; increase security; improve education; expand transport links; beautify environments; renovate buildings; infill abandoned sites; attract new investors, inventors and entrepreneurs; and hold on to the 'urban pioneers' who populate the city centres.

In London and more generally in British politics, there is now renewed concern about poverty and social exclusion and policy initiatives are being developed to try to reverse these processes. Co-ordination and partnership are seen as crucial for effective policy interventions. This issue directs attention to the form and quality of urban governance. A loss of faith in big government has led to a move to promote greater involvement of non-governmental or business agencies in decision-making and implementation – from 'government' to 'governance'. This has been part of a wider shift in politics and culture. Urban government is thus presently a key issue in debates about cities and megacities. The fragmentation of urban government has weakened responses and reduced the capacity of government to respond effectively to or plan rationally for identified risks.

How to improve urban governance? This is a key question. Since May 2000 London once again has its own government. The Mayor and Greater London Authority (GLA) has a clear statutory relationship with various functional bodies including Transport for London, the London Development Agency, the Metropolitan Police Authority, the London Fire and Emergency Planning Authority, and the Cultural Strategy Group. To what extent will the GLA be able to provide strategic co-ordination of partnership working within London to better tackle poverty and social exclusion?

Urban Leaders Survey

In 1998, the MegaCities Project[1] conducted a survey of urban leaders in New York, London, Rio de Janeiro, Tokyo, Mexico

City, New Delhi and Lagos. The survey covered leaders in business, government, academia, non-profit, labour and media. The sample was selected on positional and reputational criteria. Here I will refer briefly to some of the findings from the comparative study and then give more detail on the London results.[2]

Responses were received from 117 people in London, 90 each in Tokyo and Rio de Janeiro, 74 in New York and 73 in New Delhi with smaller numbers from the other cities. The total sample size was 545. The overall conclusions of the survey were that leaders believed they would benefit from more inter-city co-operation in solving problems, few were knowledgeable about ways in which other cities solve problems, many problems were perceived to be common to all cities, and it was thought that cities share common priorities and goals for the next few years. Some cities saw problems in their cities becoming worse while the same problems were perceived as having been successfully tackled in others. Economic development is a key priority for cities and there was a general feeling that there was not enough co-operation between the public and the private sectors.

In New York City, the decrease in the crime rate was hailed by the city's leaders as one of the most significant advances in recent years. In Rio de Janeiro, leaders complained that crime is getting worse. In Tokyo, the sense was that the economy and employment had suffered recently. Londoners felt the economic outlook had improved.

Overall however only 36% of respondents saw the quality of life in their city as being excellent or good. Views were polarised as to whether life was improving or getting worse, with 39% seeing it as getting better and 41% as getting worse. Aspects of city life seen as good included multiculturalism, jobs and education, with traffic, housing and the cost of living perceived as the worst aspects of megacity life. However overall a half felt reasonably optimistic about the future. The main issues identified commonly as priorities for action in the future were jobs and economic opportunities, educational opportunities, public transportation, housing, health care and social services, and crime and violence. Respondents all wanted better communication, information and debate about problem-solving within and between megacities. They supported ideas of co-operation and partnership.

When results from each city were compared, it was found that perceptions of the quality of life varied. In London and New York, higher percentages saw the quality of life in their city as excellent or good (56% and 69% respectively) compared to for example only 18% in Rio de Janeiro. Only 6% of London urban leaders and 3% of New York respondents thought the quality of life in their city overall to be poor or very poor while this was the case for 35% in Rio.

At the time of the survey, 79% of New York respondents thought life was getting much or somewhat better compared to only 34% of those in London: only 7% of New York leaders thought things were getting worse while this was the case for 44% of London respondents. Again comparing the two cities of New York and London, 67% of those from New York thought their city was making either a lot or some progress compared to other cities, whereas only 31% of London respondents thought so. In London 43% of respondents felt the city was falling behind other cities relatively at that time.

The areas where London respondents thought most progress had been made were in jobs and economic opportunities, city centre developments, links with other countries and cultures, starting or running a business and the overall quality of life. The areas identified where things were thought to be becoming worse were traffic congestion, public transportation, environmental quality, city government, and healthcare and other social services.

Key areas of beneficial innovation identified by London urban leaders were in regeneration, social housing, homelessness, transport, politics, funding, community and cultural life. However, there were some differences in the perceptions of different sectors as to the key examples of successful innovation:

- *Business leaders*: examples cited here included the London Docklands Development Corporation, the Covent Garden Development, refurbishment of inner city housing estates, the GLC Fares Fair policy, the creation of London First, Sunday opening, the Private Finance Initiative, the National Lottery, and changes planned for the next Census.

- *Media respondents:* singled out the Big Issue, pedestrianisation schemes, the Government Office for London, Foyer housing schemes, the GLC Fares Fair policy, the London Cycling Campaign, the new strategic authority for London, the 1950s Clean Air Act, London First, and the comprehensive estates initiatives.

- *Government respondents:* picked out the revitalised South Bank, community safety initiatives and multi-agency community partnerships, shifts in attitudes to the car, debates organised by the Evening Standard on London issues, Foyer schemes, the regeneration of Kings Cross, partnerships to address inner city decay, the manifesto for regional government promoted by the Association of London Government, summer youth programmes, Local Agenda21, and LETS schemes.

- *Community respondents*: pointed to anti-racist campaigns and also mentioned the redevelopment of the South Bank, Operation Welwyn at Kings Cross, tenant management organisations and housing associations, neighbourhood mediation and parent support programmes, assistance to encourage voluntary sector groups to be more successful in accessing SRB funds, and the Rough Sleepers initiative to tackle street homelessness.

- *Academics respondents:* cited the South Bank redevelopment, the Single Regeneration Budget, the Priority Estates Project, the Big Issue, partnership schemes, traffic control measures, and community action for youth and other local groups.

- *Labour and trade union leaders*: noted training in languages for ethnic minorities, use of CCTV to improve safety, the GLC's Fares Fair policy, anti racist alliances, work with the homeless, police action on terrorism, and improved access to further education facilities.

It was notable that government, business and community respondents were more knowledgeable about regeneration and other policy initiatives and gave more detailed examples than did media, academic and trade union respondents. There is also evidence of a polarisation of views between business respondents and the rest. Business emphasised economic and property development and tended to stress 'place' more than 'people'. Community respondents stressed social and people-based initiatives. Government respondents were most knowledgeable and referred to both aspects and the need for partnership.

Community respondents gave most stress to social developments, especially those tackling racism. Problems and developments singled out by community respondents notably included racism, racial harassment, violence and discrimination. Particular examples of successful intervention with respect to racism included the major public education awareness programme including a campaign to 'kick racism out of football'. This involved a partnership between the Commission for Racial Equality, business, local authorities, community organisations and committed individuals. The campaign used visuals, posters, postcards advertising and information for schools and young people and involved high profile champions. The aim was better behaviour, changed attitudes, more tolerance and mutual respect. A further example was the TUC 'Unite Against Racism' campaign which saw the TUC operating in conjunction with anti-racist and community organisations. A music festival 'Respect', which attracted over 100,000 young people to the heart of the East End, helped build an ongoing campaign against racism, using music as a powerful medium. The process of organising the festival brought together a range of different interests and organisations within the city.

Another favoured policy programme was the Rough Sleepers Initiative which had involved government, NGOs, local government and business working in partnership. People sleeping on the streets included young vulnerable people and people with mental health problems. The initiative was coordinated by central government but implemented by a number of local authorities, housing associations and voluntary agencies. It was said to have provided £180 million in three phases to London. 1,500 self-contained , permanent homes were provided between 1994-6. It had benefits for homeless people but also for business and tourism. Street homelessness in London was said to have reduced from 2,000 per night to 350 per night.

Conclusion

What emerges from studies of London and other cities is the conclusion that the quality of decision-making is the key to success in tackling urban problems. Relations between national and city governments are also crucially important for the effectiveness of policy interventions. Currently all cities face increasing pressures from rapidly growing and diversifying populations, the retreat from the welfare state, and globalisation. In the new network society, I would argue, a new form of urban governance is becoming visible - one involving the ideology and practice of partnership (inter-sectoral, multi-agency work across departments and agencies to focus on agreed problems) and community involvement. The partnership principle involves recognition of the need for a long-term approach, the need to build in continuous evaluation and the need for flexible cultures. It builds on the experience of early initiatives such as Healthy Cities, City Challenge, Safer Cities and the Drugs Prevention Initiatives. There are however problems in implementing partnerships - problems of sharing information, (varying willingness to do so and differences in categories and systems used, methods of information collection and storage) conflicts of cultures and different perceptions of what are the key priorities. A key question is whether or not all partners are equal? And whether or not the community is included as a partner.

All these developments are changing the shape of local politics, democracy and governance and will influence the future direction of London city government as it operates within the new uncertainties of devolution. Reactions to these trends are varied. Some see them as just manipulation from above - the extension of managerialist principles into the community with a fear that communities are being dumped on by being asked to take on tasks that were previously the responsibility of paid professionals and bureaucrats. Others think that partnerships can be facilitative and creative if they involve mutual respect and others hope that they may form the base for a revival of grass roots democracy. What is evident however is that these changes have opened up new opportunities for involvement and influence and the possibility that local people might be able to make their voice heard when decisions are made that affect their lives.

Acknowledgements

Assistance on the London urban leaders survey was provided by Helen Yianni and Matthew Shirley. I should like to thank them for their good work.

Notes

[1] The MegaCities Project is a transnational, not for profit network dedicated to sharing innovative solutions to the problems of the world's largest cities. It focuses especially on issues of democracy and empowerment, poverty, women, and environmental sustainability.

[2] In the London survey, there were many non-respondents, several writing to say that they were too busy to complete the questionnaire. The response rate overall was nearly 40%. The majority of refusals came from business with community and media also presenting difficulties. The most frequent reason for refusal was that the person was too busy and some organisations said they had a policy not to complete such questionnaires for this very reason. Some of these people – high powered chief executives - sent personal letters explaining this but wishing us well. Some people rejected the concept urban leader and refused to participate for this reason. (They either felt it was too authoritarian or they did not classify themselves as leaders).

References

Castells, M. (1996) *The Rise of the Network* Society, Oxford, Blackwell.

Coote, A. (1999) 'A bill of wrongs' in *The Guardian* Wednesday February 3rd, p.7.

Lawson, R. (1993) 'Causes and scale of poverty' Paper presented at *Seminar on Old and New Poverty in the Welfare States* Friedrich Ebert Foundation, London 11-12 December.

Power, A. (1999) 'Pool of resources' in *The Guardian* Wednesday February 3rd, pp.2-3.

Chapter 10

Ethnic Business in the London Economy

RAM GIDOOMAL

Introduction

London is a richly multi-cultural society and the benefits have been mutual. Minority ethnic communities have for decades played a large part in clothing Londoners, operating on Londoners and drilling their teeth, selling Londoners milk and newspapers when other shops are closed for the day, feeding Londoners and introducing them to a variety of cuisine, collecting fares on London buses, pushing the boundaries of London's popular music ever further out, looking after London's tube system, and sitting on stools in the National Gallery making sure that no Londoner walks off with a Rembrandt.

In our turn, those of us who are members of the ethnic communities were often received into Britain as penniless refugees and found London a city where entrepreneurship could flourish and academic achievement did not depend on how much money you owned. The children in our communities, who have often spent their whole lives in Britain and have no first-hand knowledge of their country of origin, can rightfully claim to be British and they enjoy a cultural climate that is increasingly tolerant, accepting and diverse. The stress here must be on 'increasingly'; there remains much unfinished business still to do.

The Problems

In 1997, as Chairman of Race for Opportunity London, the author co-chaired a steering group mandated to create 1,000 jobs for London's ethnic minority unemployed. The research we commissioned showed that London's ethnic minority communities account for 23% of its population but generate only 15% of its annual income; £7.2 billion after tax. Those figures make a stark contrast with the numerous success stories in the ethnic minorities and the fact that a great deal of those minority communities do seem to be making a great deal of money (e.g. the Chinese own one quarter of all take-away catering outlets; ten years ago around two-thirds of all independent retail outlets were owned by South Asians). But the high profile success of certain individuals has to be viewed within a wider picture: unemployment among Blacks and Asians in 1995-6 was almost twice the rate for the whole population (LRC, 1997). The minority ethnic communities face social and economic disadvantage to a high degree.

Many of the factors contributing to this are well known. The stories of London's ethnic groups illustrate both diversity but also a degree of commonality. The South Asian communities, for example, were established in the late sixties when an influx of refugees holding British passports arrived from East Africa and other troubled regions. Many of the Jewish community arrived as refugees from Europe, during the Nazi regime and escaping even earlier pogroms and purges. African-Caribbeans arrived in large numbers in response to invitations from London Transport to work in the capital. Other communities, like the Chinese, are much longer established, but have been traditionally associated with socially low-end occupations such as laundries and fish-and-chip shops. By and large the origins of London's ethnic minorities have been in poverty and flight, social stigma and menial labour, coupled with frequent fear and prejudice from the majority population who perceived these new arrivals to be threats to their homes and jobs.

We must acknowledge that the discrepancy between numbers and gross product masks significant variations: that some sectors of the minority communities are performing above the London and even the national average, but that many others continue to struggle with disadvantage, deprivation and social exclusion. Let us consider some of the underlying issues here.

Financial structures

Although intentional discrimination undoubtedly exists, it is also worth considering unintentional deprivation caused by sheer lack of consideration and identification of new markets. Elsewhere the author has told of his own experiences helping his mother, newly arrived in the UK and as yet not fluent in English, to find a bank where the staff were able to show her how to do basic domestic banking. Today much has changed and the major banks have staff able to communicate in the major languages spoken in Britain; indeed firms like Blackstone Franks and Grant Thornton have whole divisions dealing with the business needs of the ethnic communities. But when, for example, the Better Regulation Task Force's Anti-Discrimination Legislation Working Party, examined the help currently available for the ethnic communities it recommended strongly that simplified and more accessible alternatives should be found to the mass of confusing, and often difficult to negotiate, red tape and advice which currently exists.

These issues are being taken seriously, not least by the Bank of England which has invited leading members of Britain's ethnic communities to join a series of discussions to examine funding and consider existing research on ethnic minority businesses. Currently ethnic businesses are experiencing some success but in the face of a financial system stacked against them and which requires further reform.

Employment structures

The Task Force was by no means the only organisation to identify the continuing existence of glass ceilings and wage discrimination that exists for ethnic minorities. It was a point that Tony Blair made very early on in his Prime Ministerial career when he stated: 'Not one black High Court judge; not one black chief constable or permanent secretary. Not one black army officer above the rank of colonel. Not one Asian, either. Not a record of pride for the British establishment' The problem is encountered in other minorities –women, disabled people and others – and is similarly masked by the outstanding performance of a visible few.

The Blair government continues to demonstrate commitment to this issue. The author's own experiences illustrate that the government is at least listening to business voices in the ethnic communities. As a member of the Government Office for London's Minority Ethnic Advisory Group, set up by the director of Government Office for London to examine precisely these issues; we have urged, for example, 'capacity building' – creating within the ethnic minority communities the skills and resource capacity to bid for major contracts. The author is also a member of the Ethnic Minority Advisory Group for the New Deal Task Force - a key plank in New Labour's policies - and has spoken to conferences of the Association of Chief Police Officers and the Navy Recruitment Board, on ethnic minority issues. Improving the employment possibilities of ethnic minorities is on the political agenda but the will to convert this into action still needs to be demonstrated.

Racism and prejudice

Racism is, thankfully, a largely discredited view in today's Britain, but a worrying number of people still hold racist views. London has the greatest concentration of the ethnic minority population, so racist attitudes might be expected to be more prevalent in London, not least because their high visibility leads many people to think that the numbers are higher than they are (current predictions are that ethnic minorities are approaching 10% of the population). Nevertheless, in a recent survey 19% of respondents felt that there are too many black people living in the UK, and young people, especially young males, agreed to a disturbing extent. As attitudes are known to harden with age, much needs to be done to educate youngsters against racism. The price of racism includes problems in community, in housing, in education and much more

One should emphasise, however, that the problems that face the ethnic minority businesses run much deeper than those thus far mentioned. After all, the three mentioned are familiar in most days' news items. Let us turn our attention to three that get little publicity:

The success factor

Ironically, the very success that some ethnic communities have had has worked against them. Asian shopkeepers that pioneered the idea of late night opening - my own family was one - have seen hypermarkets and large stores follow their lead with enough resources to price-slash their way into a dominant position. For example in Hammersmith supermarkets have, by extending their opening hours, killed off the local shops that created the late-night economy in the first place. Major multinational food chains are now selling ethnic food, benefiting from pioneering work by the communities that made it popular in the majority community, but employing chefs and other staff in the country of origin – thus both capturing a niche market and also creating unemployment in the ethnic communities. Such stories are common and the situation isn't helped by the fact that ethnic minorities are often dependent on family or ethnic financial input, banking and accountancy. They often maintain an illusion of security until, too late, they realise the threat.

The finance factor

This inward-looking financial structuring often creates unwieldy and unsatisfactory businesses, where grossly unsuited members of the family are given senior executive responsibilities, for no other reason than that they are members of the family, or a relative in a distant part of the world is entitled to substantial drawings from the company, but contributes no skills or experience. There are many strengths in ethnic minority business – the 'Family Council' concept, for example, has often worked well – but, when business decisions are made on a different basis than that of what is best for the company, ethnic minority businesses all too easily lose the cutting edge.

Generational and succession factors

Many of our ethnic communities, notably those whose members came to Britain in the post-war years, are now entering the second generation. This fact has considerable significance. Often with considerable sacrifice and hardship they built up businesses which enabled them to educate their children and give them a good standard of living. However, when those children come to decide their own careers, the family corner shop, laundry or chip shop is unlikely to be their first choice, and when it is, the presence of a business-literate member of a family that has run its business largely intuitively can cause frictions in itself. Add to this the problems of handing on the business to the next generation and the conflict between being fair to offspring (who may have very varying degrees of business acumen), and making the future of the business secure, is often a huge one. There are also cultural problems. Do youngsters in our ethnic communities regard themselves as being of their country of origin (which they have probably never seen), as being as British as the rest of the population, or as being 'British African', or 'British Chinese', or 'British Asian' – labels that may or may not be worn with pride?

Like the other two factors, this is not something that is widely discussed. However it is encouraging to see that some accountancy firms are creating specialist departments, training specialist staff, and providing specialist resources to address such matters as the succession issue. Furthermore, the question of ethnic identity in a new generation is to a large extent being addressed by the young people themselves. Certainly in the media and entertainment where some ethnic-flavoured TV programmes like 'Goodness Gracious Me' and 'Ali G', for example, are considered some of the most exciting and valuable products around.

These less visible factors are 'fault lines', like the dangerous geological phenomena that exist in the background for many years before a shift in local circumstances, a period of harsh climate, or a spate of local activity forces the landslide or the earthquake that has always been waiting to happen. In the meantime, at ground level, wonderful enterprises may well be going on which seem to indicate that the good times will go on forever.

The Challenge

What can be done to address the visible and invisible problems that the ethnic minority businesses face, so that the business of governing London may indeed promote competitiveness and regeneration for a global city?

Before anything else, it should be stated that we must not allow our awareness of the positive things that have been done and the progress that has been made over the past few years to obscure the fact that much still needs to be done. Much of what has been achieved so far addressed long-standing problems that go back decades. We need to go further, and address problems that are appearing now and belong to now. Problems, which, just as with the generational problems, could only have happened at this point in London's history, and therefore require new and far-sighted solutions.

Some of the answers are general in scope and call for change of attitude rather that major reform, just as in the Task Force we saw little need for new legislation but a great need for persuasion and strengthening of existing measures. For example, the Banks and financial institutions, after the advances of recent years, must strategically plan for the next phase. It is encouraging that the HSBC South Asian banking team, for example, now installs specialist managers in areas of large ethnic minority population, and that the British Bankers Association, in collaboration with the Commission for Racial Equality and various lenders, has launched a two-year study on minority ethnic funding. However more research and more rapid action on the conclusions of such research is clearly needed.

Employers must continue to fight against negative discrimination and seek out the distinctive qualities and skills of the ethnic minorities. Current views of business and management emphasise this. For example the emerging concept of corporate citizenship acknowledges that today's companies have responsibilities to the total community, including such areas as environment and social welfare. A concept of the total community that does not give due attention to the ethnic minorities has missed the point entirely.

However, these are hardly new solutions. Let us now consider two current developments in the governance of London, the London Development Agency (LDA) and the Small Business Service (SBS) which, I believe, offer new and unique opportunities to develop ethnic minority business.

The London Development Agency

The gestation period has been a long one. The first stage was the London Development Partnership (LDP), a voluntary partnership, 'to bring together all the key players in London's economy', formed with the agreement of ministers to take key strategic work forward in advance of the launch of the LDA in July 2000. Chaired by Lord Marshall, it included in the Business sector Gulam Noon, Chairman and MD of Noon Products and a substantial representative of the ethnic minorities business community.

In April 1999 the Partnership published its London Innovation and Knowledge Transfer Strategy, the result of a steering group co-led by Mr Noon. The strategy includes stimulating innovation across London, exploiting London's knowledge base, using London's innovation assets, and targeted action on key sectors and the sub-regions of London. The strategy document emphasises that 'knowledge exists in all of us and can be expanded and exploited by transferring it and then putting it to work to encourage innovation'.

The implications of such a strategy for ethnic minority communities are potentially highly significant given the immense wealth of knowledge potential in these communities. In *The UK Maharajahs* (Gidoomal, 1997) I surveyed the very high rate of ethnic-minority success in British universities and colleges, and the high take-up of industrial graduate training schemes in large multi-nationals among UK ethnic minority members. The tragedy so far has been that for many in these communities there has been lack of opportunity and incentive to develop potential. Many have left Britain to study in America or in their country of origin, and a small but significant 'brain drain' has been in effect.

The development of such a 'Knowledge Transfer Strategy' by the LDA would be important not because it is redressing past wrongs (except insofar as it makes opportunity more fairly available), but because it builds on strengths. The ethnic communities in London have vast resources we have barely begun to tap, and LDA strategies mist identify these and build upon them.

The Small Business Service

A consultation process for the SBS began in June 1999 on the basis of DTI proposals for an agency that would provide a strong voice for small firms in Government, help small firms to cope with regulation, and create integration and coherence in business support. This is a 'Gordian knot' approach to problems that have been treated with ad hoc solutions for years. It offers a crosscutting, focused approach and its radical review of small business support includes, for example, heavy use of IT and new technology in general.

The SBS is potentially good news for the minority ethnic business communities given the apparent improved awareness of ethnic business issues. The DTI (2000) response document states:

> "The SBS should promote the interests of all small businesses. This includes businesses run by women, ethnic minority businesses and businesses in deprived communities as well as businesses in more remote areas. The SBS will develop, as part of its first corporate plan, a strategy to support businesses facing particular obstacles where a particular effort is required: for example, people in the Afro-

Caribbean and other ethnic minority communities or women seeking to start or grow their own businesses. In addition, the SBS will be responsible for the £30m Phoenix fund, which is designed, among other things, to support and stimulate enterprise in deprived areas. More broadly, the DTI is setting up an Ethnic Minority Business Forum as a sounding board for the views of ethnic enterprises."

To restate, this is potentially a forward-looking solution, not a collection of remedies for old problems. It is a genuine attempt to create a new environment for UK small businesses, and it is encouraging (though no more than right and proper) that the government has listened to its advisors and to extensive feedback and built in so much provision of ethnic minority business. It remains to be seen how the franchise of the SBS in London, London Business Link, operationalises this new approach. There remains deep concern that the representation of ethnic minority communities is still low in certain important economic development institutions. To ignore such a significant sector of London population is dangerous, and we must take care to maximise ethnic minority representation.

Nobody who really understands the British ethnic minority's business potential wants charity from the government. A level playing field, minimal red tape and freedom to exploit skills is what is needed. Let us note the importance of skills in this context. The London Skills Forecasting Unit has identified various areas of skill shortages. In 1998 London had vacancies in 20% of its workplaces, 8% of which were regarded as 'difficult to fill'. Yet many of the job areas identified as needing filling called for skills that are either well-represented, or have considerable potential, in the ethnic minority communities – not least in computers and IT, where Asians and Chinese are among the world leaders. Developing skills to enable skills to be matched to vacancies is a function that any London agency starting in a new millennium must have on the top of the agenda.

The Wider Picture

The current business buzzword is 'e-commerce' – electronic commerce – and the meteoric rise of the Internet and the explosion in Internet trading has opened up huge markets and made vast fortunes for many entrepreneurs. People who were the first to identify this new market coined the 'e-commerce' term. To do this they had to identify new and unexpected motivators and workers: many of them very young, many living in remote places, very few of them looking like the traditional picture of the successful entrepreneur.

In a similar vein, I would like to advance another concept: 'g-commerce', or global commerce. G-commerce describes a concrete reality. The ethnic minority communities in Britain have huge links with the fragmented Diaspora communities of which they are part. They have existing trade links, existing financial structures and much more already in place. Successful businesses in Britain, such as the Hinduja empire, trade and invest internationally on a scale creating global cash-flow networks of the kind that some more conventional businesses spend years trying to create. British ethnic communities have access to resources, to markets, to trade contacts, to expert advisors and much more, and the majority community in Britain are barely aware of the fact. London's potential for tapping and working with this global economy to which 23% of its population have free access is immense. It's not too much to say that London can and should become the g-commerce capital of the world.

The ethnic minority communities can play a very large part in making that happen, both by contributing the skills and resources they already posses and also by contributing the many skills and resources that they would certainly develop if given the backing and support of the government in the ways we have been considering, and more.

As with e-commerce, g-commerce may hold some surprises: its most talented operators may not look like one expects them to look, especially in those boardrooms and policy making bodies where the glass ceiling is still in place and few faces from the ethnic minorities are to be seen. But the opportunity is there and the new forms of governance currently emerging in London must operate to maximise the potential of London's ethnic business communities. The issue is not, 'How can we put right the wrongs done in the past', but 'What a huge business resource the ethnic minority communities are'. Why on earth isn't London making more use of them?'

References

Department of Trade and Industry (DTI) (2000) *Responses to Consultation Document on Small Business Service*, London, DTI.

Gidoomal, R. (1997) *The UK Maharajah's*, London, Nicholas Brealey.

London Research Centre (LRC) (1997) *Cosmopolitan London*, London, London Research Centre.

Chapter 11

Expert or Lobbyist? Universities, The New Regional Agenda and London's Governance

PAUL BENNEWORTH AND DAVID CHARLES

Introduction

We are at a critical moment in the evolution of London's governance. Although Central Government has set in place the structures for London, the process of creating a new government for London is still unfolding. The first Mayor and Assembly are currently establishing working practices that will structure the subsequent evolution of the Greater London Authority (GLA). Important political choices are also being made concerning the leaders of the new institutions and the *eminences grises* who will have the particular attention of the Mayoral ear. This process is marked by a concerted effort by a range of stakeholders to influence and involve themselves in the range of changes that are taking place in the capital.

The Government has made it clear whom it believes are appropriate consultees to have influence in the 'London Project'. The White Paper, *A Mayor and Assembly for London* (1997), indicates that "minorities, trade unions, young people, small businesses" (1.19) should be considered on an individual basis, while the Mayor is statutorily bound to consult with a set of other local and London stakeholders[1]. These diverse groups and their members are already much in contact with each other through a range of pan-London and sub-regional partnership projects (DETR, 1998).

The other contributors to this book have noted that a key feature of London's governance is its complexity. The Act that created the Authority and Functional Bodies is the largest piece of legislation since the 1947 India Act (which created three separate countries). As a consequence of this complexity, the contribution of particular sectors tends to be examined only in terms of their contribution to representative groups. The main contribution of local authorities to the changes in governance could conceivably be represented as involvement of the Association of London Government. The problem with this is it overlooks local authorities involvement in other local, regional and national groups engaging with the debate around London's changing governance. There is a further risk that any analysis of the debate ignores those groups whose contribution is not statutorily encouraged, viewing their contribution only through their involvement in accredited organisations.

A range of groups are seeking to engage with the Mayor by coming together and providing a single voice where one is not mandated by statute. One clear omission from the extant maps of London governance are the direct effects of the Higher Education (HE) sector. The mainstream debate places universities as participants within particular London partnerships. It is therefore assumed that universities' interests equate with those of the partnership organisations with which they are involved. Given the complexity of the London system, it is unsurprising that universities are involved with bodies as diverse as inward investment promotion (London First), the London Development Agency and its precursor the London Development Partnership (LDP), as well as a range of local and regional partnerships.

This chapter seeks to correct this imbalance, and to examine the extent of the potential influence that higher education, as a sector within London can offer to the momentous changes underway in England's capital. The chapter begins by outlining why universities are currently overlooked in mainstream analyses of the London governance system. The chapter then turns to looks at the way in which universities are involved with London governance across three dimensions; through their roles as repositories of knowledge, as self-interested organisations and as community-centred development partners. The chapter then concludes with a discussion of what the sector has to offer the new GLA arrangement, and the steps the higher education sector in London is taking to ensure its full participation in this exciting, uncertain and politically turbulent time[2].

A Historical Perspective of Universities and Governance

Although the UK university system has its roots in the established Church, London universities were particularly important in the creation of a secular and political university sector. University College London (UCL) played a key part in this process, being founded in 1826 as a counter to the clerical monopoly over English university education (Jackson, 1999). UCL was also instrumental in the rise of technical higher education in the UK; one of the legacies of the ecclesiastical control over education was an orientation of the older universities towards professional education in the humanities (Coates, 1994). UCL challenged this hegemony in the 1850s with its creation of a chair in engineering which presaged the growth of the academic subject vital to supporting national economic success (Sutherland, 1994).

Although the Government assumed the partial responsibility for funding of universities in the UK in 1919, with the creation of the University Grants Committee, this consisted of a general subsidy for existing activities (Jackson, 1999). Universities were permitted largely to dictate their own policy agenda until well after the Second World War, when the state began to take an interest in the importance of higher education as a means of raising national competitiveness. Prior to that date, there was a particularly close link between universities and the state because universities provided the national administrative élites who took and implemented political decisions in the UK (Henkel & Little, 1999).

Even by the time of the Robbins Report into Higher Education (1963) which provided the foundation for the first wave of the expansion of higher education, universities were still seen as an important contributor to the national system of governance (Robbins, 1963; Smith, 1999). During this period of expansion, universities were well-organised as a group and sought to retain control over their own activities. An unfortunate by-product of this process was that academics as a group became regarded by government as driven by self-interest and self-preservation, undermining their claim to provide a broad service to society (Van Ginkel, 1994). This led to the later Dearing Inquiry into Higher Education (1997) to underline the cultural and social mission for universities to "play a major role in shaping a democratic, civilised, inclusive society".

A parallel problem was the fact that besides the erosion of universities' independence by the state, the idea of what universities were for increasingly became identified with the provision of teaching. Even with rising interests in notions of learning societies, universities were stereotyped as providers of a highly skilled workforce, meeting graduate labour market needs (Goddard, 1999). Although research was an important element of university activity, in the 1990s, the purpose of this was consolidated around a heavily instrumentalist economic discourse, with the sole rationale of raising national competitiveness through improving the scientific base (Henkel & Little, 1999). The 1990s analyses of the universities' social contribution owe much to the American model of providing equality through access to education rather than providing a common cultural benchmark for a society (Harvie, 1994; Keohane, 1999). Taking this to its natural conclusion, universities would become quasi-public agencies, delivering education and research in line with Government policies (Jackson, 1999).

This changing understanding of the fundamental purpose of universities is highly worrying, because although it is clear universities have an economic role, an important element of a learning society is the power of critique and self-analysis (Barnett, 1995). "The university must be free to question fashion and undermine consensus where this is perceived to be mistaken. It will serve the interests of the country better if it...has a role in the transmission of knowledge and the maintenance of a culture that goes far beyond the present concerns of government" (p.175).

Civil Service reorganisation in the 1980s left the newly formed Department for Education and Employment a very centralised and powerful organisation, keen to use education as a tool of social control. Latterly, this has resulted in frequent criticisms of researchers deviating from the Government's political discourses (Jackson, 1999; DfEE, 2000). Although universities could in the past be criticised for their lack of innovation and unwillingness to change, excessive bureaucratisation of research (particularly in policy spheres) threatens to create what JS Mill called the 'pedantocracy'; a society in which stability not creativity is the fundamental driver (Jackson, 1999; Landes, 1999). This Civil Service reorganisation also left research funding under the control of the DTI, which accounts for the concentration on the contribution of science to competitiveness alluded to above.

Universities are key players in a number of policy networks, although increasing central control of education agendas has reduced their influence. A further barrier has been their relative failure, until recently, to organise and articulate themselves as anything approximating a sector, either at a national or regional level (Benneworth, 1999). The universities position as autonomous bodies hindered their co-operation and delayed the creation of a formal grouping, the Committee of Vice-Chancellors and Principals. Latterly, however, this situation has come under pressure, nationally from increasing commonalities of interest arising from falling real funding levels, and regionally from the creation of regional institutional tiers (Chatterton & Goddard, 1999).

This discussion of the purposes of universities indicates that there are a number of dimensions along which universities can contribute to this changing governance system within London. A very important element of this is the contribution that the universities make to the delivery of the learning elements contained in the objectives of pan-London bodies and local partnerships. Universities also have a role to play in producing an intellectually aware and politically sophisticated London population, ensuring that all sections of the community have access to the political and social benefits of a university education. However, universities also are important actors in this whole process of changing governance. Although regarded as government agencies, the London universities are diffuse and collegial bodies with enormous potential as political actors to shape the process of change. It is to this potential and emerging political behaviour by universities that this chapter now turns.

The London Universities - Reflexive Thinking and Political Activity

Limiting their involvement to a purely functional level would represent a huge lost opportunity for the London universities. As a consequence of that realisation, universities have devoted considerable effort to making sure that their voices are heard as the new London system of governance evolves. However, the problem in the past for universities was not only that they did not choose to engage with regional policy networks, but that there were systematic barriers to their engagement. There is some appreciation amongst the London universities that both these structural and institutional problems inhibited effective contribution and participation in forums which could use their special expertise and experiences to shape the change process for the greater good.

Individuals within universities have for a long time been contributing to the debates around the future for London, and have proven instrumental in facilitating new ideas. However, in the main this has been in an *ad hominem* and departmental capacity, without systematic strategies for formalising or institutionalising the process. Unique to London is the relationships between the post-1992 universities and local authorities. Many former polytechnics outside London retain close links to their host local authorities as a vestige of their former municipal status. The absence of this within London means that the post-1992 sector is less constrained; in London, many of the local authorities are close collaborators across district boundaries, so universities are involved both with local authorities and with partnership consortia.

It is increasingly true that universities are writing their strategies mindful of the requirement for regional engagement, the third priority for the HE sector nationally. In the context of the current changes in London, this requires informing and shaping the debate around the institutions and the civil society structures necessary to successfully bed in the GLA. Involvement by the universities requires they act as a coherent sector suitable for consultation. The net effect of this has been to increase the degree of local and regional engagement by the London universities, not merely in delivery of teaching, training and social inclusion, but contributing to shaping important social and political debates around the nature of London society.

This section of the chapter examines these areas in some more detail. First, we say a little more about the degree to which universities have contributed to debates about London (e.g. through the *The City Research Project*, *The London Study* and *London: A Global City* report). The following section then looks at the way in which universities have sought to organise themselves as a sector, and to modify the perceptions of their interests. Particularly notable is the fact that universities have intentionally repositioned themselves as business-type organisations, in line with Government desires, rather than waiting to have that change forced upon them from the centre. Finally, the paper looks at the way that universities have sought to present their interests politically, with the creation of the London Higher Education Consortium (LHEC), driven by a regional Higher Education Funding Council for England (HEFCE) agenda, but aiming to give a voice for the HE sector in the new London-region institutions.

Universities as conduits for specialist knowledge

It is necessary to say at the outset that it would be highly inaccurate to portray London's universities as individually or jointly remote from the governance agenda. Although there are systematic barriers to the inclusion of the universities formally in certain policy networks, particular research groups and individuals within London universities have for a long time been instrumental in providing intellectual support for the development of particular policy areas. Furthermore, it is also true that these relationships will continue to be important into the future, despite efforts to systematise communications and negotiations between universities and the state.

One particular area of note in which universities have played a great role is in the formal planning process, which has been one of the areas in which the coherence of London as a city has been maintained in the inter-regnum between the GLC and the GLA. A range of institutions, the Bartlett School of University College, the London School of Economics, the London Business School and the Local Economy Policy Unit (of South Bank University) have all been involved in providing high-quality planning research on a cross-city basis despite the lack of a London tier of government.

The London universities have also been closely involved in the political research, analysis and critique process surrounding the Mayor. Because the Mayoral idea emerged relatively late in the Labour Manifesto process (lacking the pedigree of the Scottish Parliament or Welsh Assembly), much of the engagement has been reactive, as information about the nature of the new London systems have emerged. Thus, the Constitution Unit (CU) specifically omitted consideration of Mayors from their pre-election report on Regional Government in England (1996), and noted the main issue for London was resolving the tension with the rest of the South East. However, the CU and indeed the London universities more generally, have a great deal of long-term expertise, knowledge and understanding of the highly complex London governance system.

Universities as businesses and employers

It is interesting that in the statutory documents establishing the GLA, there is no mention of the London HE institutions as comprising a coherent sector, and hence deserving recognition and consultation. However, much importance is given to consultation with the business and wealth-creating sector. It is therefore perhaps unsurprising that some universities have chosen to stress their contribution to the creation of wealth as a means of having their voice heard. Indeed, some universities have gone so far as to join business-led organisations as a way of demonstrating their commitment to being, and hence value as, commercially-aware organisations.

Of particular interest are those universities which have involved themselves with the representatives of the business sector. Indeed, a number of HE institutions have sought to stress they are not merely educators of graduates, but because of their budgets, employment and commercialisation activities, active contributors to the economy.

London First is the Regional Development Office for London, supporting the attraction and embedding of inward investment in London, and uniquely amongst the English RDOs, it is not incorporated by statute into its regional Development Agency, the LDA. 19 London universities have to date joined London First, and join some 300 other businesses and support organisations with an interest in the promotion of London as a global city. This is clearly in the universities' interests, because they have an interest in the attraction of overseas students, but also because it provides the infrastructure to represent universities, but with the cachet of business leadership that a private-sector led organisation can offer.

One of the services that London First provides for its members is support for any sub-group of members who feel that a piece of research might contribute to supporting the case of London as a globally networked and competitive city. With 19 members from the HE sector, a University sub-grouping made sense, and 'Learning in London' (LIL) was duly formed to fulfil that role, to put forward a business-led voice of the London research community. Although restricted to promotional activities, LIL is noteworthy because it specifically addresses the criticisms of self-interest and introspection that are continually levelled at universities. LIL is significant in that it is one element of a broader thrust of university involvement, encompassing both the LDP/LDA and the LHEC.

Universities as a coherent, politically-active sector

Although LIL seeks to represent the research community in London, it is not a formal grouping of the senior executives of the

London HE sector. It is therefore limited in its scope of activity, and relies to a great degree on the presence of other organisations to create a united voice for universities. This role is fulfilled by the London Higher Education Consortium (LHEC), a voluntary association which exists to represent London's universities to any organisation with a regional interest, including HEFCE, LIL and the GLA. There were two main drivers in the formation of LHEC, neither of which were directly stimulated by the creation of the London Authority, but which have provided universities with the capacity to engage with the new Authority.

The first driver was an entirely separate agenda coming out of HEFCE, who have recently encouraged universities to think more about their regional co-operation, appointing regional consultants to facilitate this process in each region. Dearing recommended that HEFCE encourage the formation of regional consortia following the North East model to co-ordinate service delivery and collaboration in infrastructure costs. Consequently, HEFCE have been encouraging each region to establish a consortium to represent regional HE interests. London has been a late mover in this process, in part because of the complexity of co-ordinating a body of such size and complexity (in contrast the corresponding body in the North East has only six members) and LHEC was not launched until March 2000.

The second driver was an increasing *de facto* involvement of university executives in a range of London-wide activities, and the realisation by these individuals that their position would be much stronger if backed as a united voice for the HE sector. Professor Roderick Floud, for example, joined the LDP board as an 'expert' from the HE sector, but the collective support of LHEC have made him a great deal more influential in the process of drafting a London Regional Economic Strategy than as a co-opted representative. Indeed, as convenor of LHEC, Professor Floud has a wide remit to represent the HE sector to other London agencies. Other members of the LDP board were also keen for Floud to be seen to be speaking on behalf of the higher education sector.

LHEC provides a capacity for universities to respond to other emerging agendas on a London-wide basis. LHEC has subsequently taken a lead in co-ordinating bids for central DfEE funds for business and community engagement, and has succeeded in winning two projects collectively in support of this. This provides the coherence to the regional engagement, and reinforces the message that universities are more than just sources of graduates and new products for businesses.

Discussion and Concluding Remarks

Universities have their own regional agenda, which, although driven by central government, is providing a motivation (and some supporting funding) for universities to focus their engagement more regionally. This has serendipitously arrived at a time when there is significant political change in London. It is natural therefore that universities should seek to use this new capacity, stimulated by their own regionalisation incentives, to engage with the GLA, and to influence policy areas, the policy debates, and indeed the political foundations on which the Authority is based. The GLA is not the only new regional body which will affect universities, and to which this regionalisation process is relevant; the new Learning and Skills Councils and Small Businesses Services will all benefit from the HE sector having a single voice in London.

However, of the plethora of political and institutional changes underway in the capital, none is more important than the new Authority. By providing an ear for the universities, it has stimulated the emergence of bodies speaking regionally, which together provide a genuinely strategic capacity for their host regions. The capacity is not derived solely from one organisation, neither from LHEC, nor LDP nor LIL, rather this capacity comes from a change in the way that universities pursued a number of strategic directions in response to a variety of stimuli. The universities have chosen to work together to produce a coherent voice for the sector as well as providing mechanisms for strategic co-operation with other sectors.

Political events have reinforced the vernacular understanding that the GLA is not a beefed-up local authority, but a regional authority on a par with the Scottish Parliament or the Welsh Assembly[3]. Universities clearly have a role to play in shaping and educating a civil society about this novel and uncertain third tier of government in between, and to some degree subordinate to, local and national government. This is more in line with their traditional role as independent bodies supporting the development of a common intellectual conception of citizenship, rather than quasi-state bodies delivering centrally-stipulated services.

Universities are not merely self-interested lobbyists attempting to maximise the financial benefits they can derive from the new system of governance for London. Rather, their expertise, generated through inter-related education and research on local, national and international scales is a positive and dynamic asset for other London policy actors. Furthermore, through this education, research and community involvement, universities have proven themselves important social, economic and environment players in London. Although the complexity of the situation might serve to hide the contribution made by universities, it is clear that they have critical economic, political and social roles to fulfil in delivering regeneration, social inclusion and competitiveness as current changes to London's governance unfold.

Notes

[1] The Mayor is bound by the GLA Bill to consult formally with organisations representing four sectors, "a) voluntary bodies some or all of whose activities benefit the whole or part of Greater London; (b) bodies which represent the interests of different racial, ethnic or national groups in Greater London; (c) bodies which represent the interests of different religious groups in Greater London; (d) bodies which represent the interests of persons carrying on business in Greater London." (GLA Bill 1999 para 27(3))

[2] The research for this chapter was carried out under the European Commission-funded TSER UNIREG Project by the Centre for Urban and Regional Development Studies. The authors would like to thank the

interviewees for the research work, who were drawn from a range of Universities, representative bodies (*inter alia* LDP, LHEC, LF), as well as key individuals involved in the GLA Transition Team, Romney House, London.

[3] Evidence of this comes through the amendments made to the 2000 Representation of the People Bill, in which provision exists for all the candidates for Mayor to have a free mailing to every voting household. This is akin to elections for the Scottish Parliament and Welsh Assembly rather than to local (district) authorities.

References

Barnes, J. (1999) 'Funding and university autonomy' in M. Henkel, & B. Little (eds) *Changing Relationships Between Higher Education and the State*, London, Jessica Kingsley.

Barnett, R. (1995) 'Universities for a learning society' in F. Coffield (ed) *Higher Education in a Learning Society*, Durham, Durham University School of Education.

Benneworth, P.S. (1999) 'The future for relations between Higher Education and RDAs' *Regions*, 220, pp.15-22.

Chatterton, P. & Goddard, J. B. (1999) 'Regional Development Agencies and the knowledge economy: harnessing the potential of universities' *Environment & Planning C: Government and Policy*, vol.17, no.6, pp.685-700.

Coates, D. (1994) *The Question of UK Decline: the Economy, State and Society*, Hemel Hempstead, Harvester Wheatsheaf. The Constitution Unit (1996) *Regional Government in England*, London, The Constitution Unit. Department for Education and Employment (2000) 'Blunkett rejects anti-intellectualism and welcomes sound ideas'. *DfEE Press Release 43/00*, 2nd February 2000.

Department of Environment, Transport and the Regions (1997) *A Mayor and Assembly for London*, London, The Stationary Office.

Department of Environment, Transport and the Regions (1998) *Building Partnerships in the English Regions: A Study Report of Regional and Sub-Regional Partnerships in England*, London, The Stationary Office.

Ginkel, H. van (1994) 'University 2050: the organisation of creativity and innovation' in National Commission on Education (eds) *Universities in the Twenty-First Century - A Lecture Series*, London, National Commission on Education.

Goddard, J. B. (1999) 'How universities can thrive locally in a global economy' in H. Grey (ed) *Universities and the Creation of Wealth*, Buckingham, Open University Press.

Harvie, C. (1994) *The Rise of Regional Europe*, London, Routledge

Henkel, M. and Little, B. (1999) *Changing Relationships Between Higher Education and the State*, London, Jessica Kingsley.

Jackson, R. (1999) 'The university, government and society' in D. Smith and A-K. Langslow (eds) *The Idea of a University*, London, Jessica Kingsley.

Keohane, N. O. (1999) 'The American campus: from colonial seminary to global multiversity' in D. Smith and A-K. Langslow (eds) *The Idea of a University*, London, Jessica Kingsley.

Landes, D. (1997) *The Wealth and Poverty of Nations*, London, Little, Brown & Co.

Robbins, Lord (1963) *Higher Education: Report of the Committee 1961-1963*, London, HMSO.

Smith, D (1999) 'The changing idea of a university' in D. Smith and A-K. Langslow (eds) *The Idea of a University*, London, Jessica Kingsley.

Sutherland, S. (1994) 'The idea of a university' in National Commission on Education (eds) *Universities in the Twenty-First Century – A Lecture Series*, London, National Commission on Education.

Chapter 12

Governing London: Challenges for the New Economic Governance

STEPHEN SYRETT AND ROBERT BALDOCK

Introduction

The move over the last decade towards new forms of multi-level, multi-sectoral networked governance has created a complex, messy and often bewildering landscape in London. With power diffused across a plethora of agencies, institutions and programmes, actors in the field of economic development and regeneration are often left feeling bemused and confused as they struggle to understand the nature of the process in which they are engaged. The experience whilst unnerving can also be liberating; providing a host of new spaces for action and engagement previously denied by more centralised and hierarchical governance systems.

The unfolding of current developments in the economic governance system of London suggest new possibilities for a more strategic, integrated, democratic and transparent system. They also present new dangers for further fragmentation, contestation and duplication. The preceding chapters explain and illustrate the variety of possible outcomes from this multi-faceted process. Despite the diversity of the contributions there are some notable areas of common agreement, particularly with respect to the importance of recognising the uniqueness of the London context and in the identification of a number of key governance challenges. The rest of this final chapter will address these points and explore the issues they raise for the future development of London's governance.

The London Context

The London economy is markedly different from other UK city-regions in terms of its size, complexity, international role and economic dynamism. The competitive basis of London is based on a unique set of agglomeration economies with a labour market characterised by a high degree of flexibility, advanced skills and the presence of key decision makers (Gordon, chapter two). At the same time, London contains some of the worst areas of multiple deprivation within Britain. The governance challenge in this context is to ensure the long term competitiveness of high growth sectors operating in increasingly competitive global markets, whilst also tackling the problems of marginalised groups and localities which currently remain excluded from the benefits of processes of economic growth. In this respect the challenge is, as Clark (chapter four) points out, for London to use its own wealth to tackle its own poverty.

The functional interdependence of the London economy into the wider South East, as well as its key role in the UK national and the emerging global economy, means that key decisions relating to London's economic development are taken routinely at national and international levels (e.g. levels of public investment in transport infrastructures, UK membership of the European single currency etc.). Pan-London strategies therefore must be multi-level in conception; informed by these wider regional, national and international contexts as well as sensitive to sub-regional difference. To achieve this requires an extensive and sophisticated capacity to gather, process and respond to large scale information flows, as well as an ability to engage directly with actors at national and international levels in order to represent, and lobby for, London's interest. London's recent system of economic governance has been profoundly limited in its ability to meet these types of governance challenges. It has lacked a unified voice, democratic accountability and pan-London mechanisms for planning and co-ordinating the myriad of partnerships responsible for delivering economic development and regeneration activity. More positively it has broadened the range of actors participating in such activity and promoted new forms of co-operation and collaboration across the public, private, voluntary and community sectors (MacGregor, chapter nine).

The creation of the GLA does provide an opportunity to address these weaknesses and build upon existing strengths. However, its ability to develop a strategic and leading role for economic development and regeneration activity within London remains heavily constrained. First, for the lead economic development agency, the LDA, there are a number of important areas where it has responsibility but not direct control over implementation (e.g. SBS, LSCs, European funding, planning), a situation which limits its ability to integrate and co-ordinate economic development policy. Second, the ability of the GLA more generally to co-ordinate economic development activity with other areas of activity (e.g. housing, education, transport, investment etc.) remains restricted given that key funding streams or policy levers either lie outside of its remit altogether, or it has only partial control. As Clark (chapter four) argues, the economic development toolbox for London is limited in extent, most notably in the area of financial and fiscal measures. With central government transfers dominant, it is central government that remains the principal initiator of economic development within London. This situation will only change if there is large scale reform of the mechanisms of public funding at the sub-national level. For the GLA to develop its strategic role, it needs fiscal and financial capabilities that it currently lacks. Only when it has the ability to generate revenues and reinvest via a long term financial strategy at appropriate moments in the business cycle, will there be greater scope for strategic, long term economic development.

Governance Challenges

The contributions in this volume have identified a number of important governance challenges to be faced within London. Particularly important is the capacity of governance arrangements to develop a pan-London strategic vision, integrate and co-ordinate economic development and regeneration activity, manage sub-regional competition, and improve democratic accountability.

Strategic vision

Few would disagree that London's economic development would benefit from greater strategic vision. The challenge for London's remodelled governance system is its capacity to develop and lead an inclusive strategic vision that has broad based support. The vision put forward by the LDP (the forerunner to the LDA) in its economic strategy document stated:

> "We seek to build a London in which quality of life, protection of key environmental resources, social harmony and economic prosperity go hand in hand, reinforcing each other rather than conflicting. It will also be a London in which public, private and voluntary sectors work together to promote the diverse goals of sustainable development for the capital, forging partnerships at city-wide, sub-regional and local levels to tackle the key problems facing employers, employees, deprived communities and London's environment" (LDP, 2000: p.4).

The LDA in its draft economic strategy eschews presenting a vision statement but outlines its mission: (i) to develop and enhance London as a world centre for business; (ii) to ensure that London's strengths are used to promote the regeneration of its disadvantaged communities; (iii) to ensure that economic opportunity is open to all London citizens; and (iv) to ensure that London's development is socially, economically and environmentally sustainable (LDA, 2000: p.8).

The tenor of these statements point to an emphasis on 'balanced development' within London, in line with the current national economic development and regeneration policy agenda which promotes an integrated economic, social and environmental approach. In this respect the initial signs are that the economic strategy for London will not be dominated entirely by a business led agenda as some commentators feared. There is acceptance that economic and employment growth will not by itself benefit London's socially excluded as well as a genuine desire to engage with issues of equality and social inclusion. Such a commitment reflects growing concern about the negative social and economic consequences of rising social inequalities and recognition that London's ethnic diversity is one of its potential principal economic assets (Gidoomal, chapter ten). However, the mechanisms by which the benefits of competitive success are to be extended more widely across groups, areas and sectors in a manner that will not hinder economic dynamism, remain unclear. More vague still is the 'sustainability' agenda, with emphasis in the draft economic strategy placed on the development of an 'ongoing debate' concerning the form and process involved in moving London towards a more sustainable future (LDA, 2000; p.62).

Yet as Thornley (chapter, five) points out, the pursuit of balanced, consensual development presents its own difficulties. Whilst current 'Third Way' thinking is keen to stress the potential 'win-win' situations in the pursuit of economic competitiveness, social cohesion and environmental sustainability, it has little to say about the 'lose-lose' situations, where conflicts of interest lead to deadlock and a loss of the trust and co-operation so central to partnership working. On these issues (e.g. the expansion of Heathrow; the redevelopment of Kings Cross, plus many smaller scale sub-regional issues) London's past governance system has failed to respond, resulting in delay and uncertainty. However, given the lack of attention to issues of conflict and the procedures necessary to resolve them, it is not clear that London's modified governance system will be any better placed to cope with such issues in the future.

Developing an inclusive strategic vision for London presents a number of difficulties. Several of the contributors voice fears that key groups will be marginalised in this process. Colenutt (chapter eight) articulates this danger in terms of a two-tier London where a pan London economic development strategy is largely divorced from local and community based regeneration activity. It remains to be seen what mechanisms will be put in place to ensure that the strategy building process is inclusive, transparent and responsive to sub-regional or local needs. In the development of the LDP strategy there was an active attempt to include a range of interest groups through the setting up of various working groups. The LDA also undertook a series of consultation meetings on its own draft strategy in early 2001. Yet whilst there is a legal requirement for the GLA to consult with a number of groups, as Benneworth and Charles (chapter 11) illustrate with regard to education, this does not include certain important sectors. The difficulties of building a strategy that achieves broad based support in a region as complex and diverse as London, are profound. Newman (chapter three) points out that the problems of finding functional lead institutions acceptable to the multiplicity of other interests, is a common cause of failure in inter-institutional co-operation and in the establishment of a consensus around wider regional goals. Furthermore, there are a number of fundamental tensions in seeking to develop consensus and engage with representatives across many sectors, not least the danger of producing bland policy documents and political quick fixes in order to keep all interests 'on board'.

The extent of the strategic vision of the GLA and LDA for economic development is strongly directed by the legislative role prescribed by the GLA Act and RDA Act. However, it remains to be seen how far the GLA and LDA will move into areas where they have no direct responsibilities for the production of strategic plans, but which are critical to the future development of London's economy. Current concerns over the lack of affordable housing in London for groups on low incomes as well as the continuing poor quality of schools, have already prompted the Mayor to take an active interest in these areas. It is therefore likely that issues such as housing and education will move on to the economic development and regeneration agenda, although the lack of control over policy and funding in such areas will limit the ability to deliver strategy in these areas.

Integration and co-ordination

The lack of policy integration and co-ordination in London has resulted in considerable duplication, confusion and competition in the design and delivery of economic development initiatives. Whilst the GLA provides an opportunity to move towards more 'joined-up' action, in the area of economic development and regeneration the extent of existing fragmentation interlinked with the myriad of public, private, voluntary and community sector organisations, makes this problematic. As a result of its legislative basis and its constrained powers, the GLA must operate in partnership with a wide range of agencies to deliver its strategic role. Yet the current governance arrangements open up a series of potential areas for contestation both within the GLA (e.g. between the Mayor/Mayor's cabinet, the Assembly and the LDA), as well as between the GLA and central and local government, GOL, and the array of other economic development and regeneration agencies.

The LDA's rapidly produced draft economic development strategy begins the process of bringing together economic development activity in London by articulating nine key policy objectives (LDA, 2000)[1]. However the mechanisms by which these diverse policy objectives will be co-ordinated and integrated in practice require further elaboration and specification. More widely within the GLA there is a critical need to co-ordinate the economic development strategy with other strategies, particularly the spatial development and transport strategies, as these are central to physical regeneration activity and the development of 'regeneration gateways' in areas characterised by clusters of deprived neighbourhoods.

Externally, given that local-central tensions dominate the history of London government, the nature of the emerging relationships between the GLA and central government and GOL is particularly important. The extent to which central government works with the GLA, or seeks to exert direct control and bypass it altogether, remains to be seen. Similarly important, as Bailey (chapter seven) and Colenutt (chapter eight) point out, is the relationship of the GLA with local authorities and sub-regional partnerships. The metropolitan/municipal split under the GLA Act means that local authorities retain their planning powers and control over various functions related to regeneration (e.g. local housing, industrial estates, education and their leadership role in local partnerships). In general London's local authorities have been strongly supportive of the creation of the GLA, however the London Boroughs have real concerns about a potential loss of power to the regional level, as well as their own ability to work together in pursuit of a wider agenda.

In a number of areas the nature of working relationships with existing bodies (e.g. GOL, LSCs, SBS, London First, the London

Tourist Board etc.) remains, at the time of writing, in need of clarification. The creation of a separate regional development agency for London also necessitates close working with the South East Economic Development Agency and the East of England Development Agency, if the integrated nature of many of the region's economic issues are to be addressed. Crucially important therefore is the ongoing elucidation of responsibilities, lead agencies and the nature of working relationships within a governance system characterised by flux and considerable potential for contestation. Whilst the LDA is clearly aware of its role in agenda setting, consensus building and co-ordination (LDA, 2000, p.7) there remains no blueprint as to how this role is to be carried forward.

Sub-regional competition

In order to avoid the inefficiency of internal competition which has become an established feature of the economic development process since the mid-1980s, the London region needs to work as a collective whole, combining various strands of programmes and policies operating at appropriate spatial scales within an overall London-wide framework. However it remains doubtful the extent to which the new governance structures will be able to achieve this. Despite considerable goodwill towards the GLA, the competitive policy environment of national government policies remains largely intact and sub-regional groupings will continue to exercise their power to gain access to scarce resources.

One potential strength is that the LDA has responsibility for administering London's SRB budget, providing the possibility for a more strategic approach to the allocation of these regeneration monies on a London-wide scale. However, other regeneration funds, such as the EU Structural Funds and the New Deal for Communities, remain outside of the LDA's control under the auspices of GOL. The Mayor and LDA will therefore have to work closely with GOL in ensuring the strategic co-ordination and integration of regeneration funding in London. Furthermore, given the uncertainty over the future of the SRB, precisely what regeneration funds the LDA will control in the future remains in doubt.

Institutional change has led to a period of flux in the political landscape of London. The new boundaries of the five LSCs represent a significant realignment of London's sub-regional regeneration policy, with the large Central and Western areas confirming their importance, and most notably an expanded East ensuring the increased strategic importance of the Thames Gateway region. This process has already produced notable shifts in power, considerable competition, and new areas of co-operation, between changing sub-regional partnerships as they jockey for position in the reformulated London governance structure.

This highly politicised restructuring process has inevitably produced a number of contentious outcomes. The apparent losers are the smaller North and South London LSC areas which are in danger of being seen as peripheral in terms of both their size (the North of London comprises only four local authorities) and outer London locations. These areas are increasingly overshadowed by an East-West axis which requires the management of sprawl in the West and extensive development in the East (Sorenson, chapter six). The major winner is the Thames Gateway, a priority region for both central government and the GLA - although given this region extends beyond the GLA boundaries, regeneration here raises further issues concerning the nature of co-operation with neighbouring RDAs, as well as with central government, local authorities and sub-regional partnerships.

Alongside sub-regional restructuring around LSC boundaries, local authorities continue to lobby for their local interests through their Assembly members, and exhibit increasing tendencies to work in partnership in the pursuit of common interests. These sub-regional groupings are therefore set to play a growing role in ensuring that factors specific to their localities are addressed by the GLA. It remains to be seen the extent of sub-regional battles for supremacy over London's regeneration policy and the sustainability of arbitrary LSC areas. For the GLA engagement with these increasingly powerful sub-regional partnerships (both elected and non-elected) will be a major challenge as it seeks to promote strategic pan-London development yet retain the support of organised sub-regional groupings with divergent interests. The danger is that such a context will encourage the pursuit of short-term pragmatic political fixes to the detriment of the longer-term pan-London interest.

The democratic challenge

The link between the democratic process and regeneration activity in London was weakened from the mid 1980s by the abolition of the GLC and the creation of a variety of government appointed bodies and partnerships which had little, or no, democratic accountability. The creation of the GLA, with an elected Mayor responsible for economic development and regeneration and an elected Assembly to scrutinise the Mayor's actions, therefore marks a significant move towards redressing this democratic deficit. Yet there remains scepticism concerning the degree of democratic accountability provided by the new governance arrangements. The limited power of the Mayor and GLA in promoting economic development necessarily limits this link to the democratic process. Significant elements of economic development activity will still be delivered locally by non-elected bodies (such as local LSCs, the SBS, various partnerships etc.) with central government departments still in control of policy levers and funding streams.

The ability of the Mayor, GLA and London Assembly to create a new political sensibility within London which promotes participation, transparency, equality and co-operation, will play a central role in providing the necessary context in which a model of strategically directed networked governance can thrive. The role of the Mayor is particularly crucial. A strong and credible Mayor will facilitate the working relationships between various economic development agencies, the LDA, the Assembly, and the London Boroughs, in the pursuit of a broader economic development strategy. The Mayor also plays a vital role in lobbying and working with central government on London's behalf and promoting issues through the media.

Given the centrality of the Mayor's role, the importance placed upon economic development issues by the Mayor is significant. Mayor Livingstone has a clear understanding of the economic development and regeneration agenda in London, however other areas, most notably transport, are the Mayor's immediate 'hands-on' concern. In this context it appears likely that in the short term at least, the Mayor will give the LDA a degree of freedom to develop the economic development agenda. Inside the GLA the extent to which the Mayor will work with the Assembly and the various committees linked to it remains unclear. Early experiences (e.g. over the closure of Ford at Dagenham) indicate the Mayor's approach has been to try to work with the Assembly and develop a non-confrontational form of operation. However, ultimately the nature of this relationship will need to be examined when more divisive issues are under consideration.

For the LDA, a central question is the extent to which this form of RDA will derive greater legitimacy, and with it greater power, from its status as an agency of a directly elected Mayor. The LDA's link to the electoral process could be important in providing it with the legitimacy to provide strong leadership to a networked form of governance. Legitimacy derived from the democratic process might also permit the LDA to partially offset some of its limitations, perhaps allowing it to extend its role into related areas (e.g. housing and education) which might remain off limits to other RDAs. In this respect the success or otherwise of the arrangements in London are of wider importance as it is likely that experiences here will strongly influence the process of establishing other elected assemblies in the English regions and the future direction of the other RDAs. Yet democratic legitimacy without on the ground success will count for little. In this respect the pressure is on the LDA to prove itself, a task which will require the rapid development of an appropriate staff base, a cohesive institutional culture, and a clear vision of its role,

Final Thoughts

This volume has focused upon the changes in governance structures currently underway in London and whether these are likely to impact positively upon the previous shortcomings evident within the governance of economic development and regeneration activity within London. The governance challenges outlined in this final chapter are heavily interlinked - the pursuit of a strategic vision for London necessarily requires greater co-ordination of agencies, improved policy integration and more co-operation across boundaries, legitimated through a degree of political accountability. Responding to these challenges will be a long term process. It will also be an uncertain one, partly because of the rapidly changing external economic environment and partly because complex and messy arrangements are being developed within a pre-existing complex and messy governance context.

Economic development in London may have a new institutional infrastructure but the development of the system of economic governance is one of evolution rather than revolution. Strong lines of continuity are evident, whether in terms of the longstanding historical tensions between local and central government within London, or more immediately in terms of the actors and staff who will people the new governance arrangements. The overall effectiveness of this system will emerge out of the interaction of the London political context, national constitutional circumstances and external economic forces. More mongrel than pedigree, few would design the current economic governance system in its present form. However, mixed breeding does bring with it certain advantages. Despite the problems of the 1980s and 1990s, there were positive improvements in this period. An emphasis on partnership working, encouraging greater community based participation and recognition of the importance of diversity are all aspects present within the current governance system which are there to be built upon. It remains to be seen whether this legacy combined with the new institutional structures will permit the development of the strong, strategic leadership role combined with flexibility, inclusiveness and diversity, that is needed to manage the economic realities of a complex and rapidly changing global city.

Notes

[1] The nine key policy objectives of the LDA's (2000) draft economic strategy comprise: promoting London as a place for people and business; sustaining the London city region; meeting London's key challenges; improving business competitiveness; encouraging economic diversity;

prioritising knowledge and learning; empowering London's communities and helping disadvantaged people into work; developing the sustainable world city; and strengthening London's capacity to deliver.

References

London Development Agency (LDA) (2000) *Draft Economic Strategy*, London, LDA.

London Development Partnership (LDP) (2000) *Building London's Economy: A Strategy for the Mayor and the London Development Agency*, London, LDP.

Index